THE P ...
NORTHE... ...

MICHAEL C. HOWARD

AND

WATTANA WATTANAPUN

SILKWORM BOOKS

© 2001 by Silkworm Books
Photos, unless credited, © by Michael C. Howard
Drawings © by Wattana Wattanapun

ISBN 974-88325-1-1

This edition is first published in 2001 by

Silkworm Books
104/5 Chiang Mai–Hot Road, M. 7, T. Suthep, Muang,
Chiang Mai 50200, Thailand
E-mail address: silkworm@loxinfo.co.th

Typeset by Silk Type in Garamond 11 pt.
Cover illustration © by Wattana Wattanapun
Printed in Thailand by O. S. Printing House, Bangkok

CONTENTS

CHAPTER 1

INTRODUCTION

The name Palaung is of Burmese origin and refers to a group of Mon-Khmer speaking peoples scattered throughout the mountains of Shan State and southern Kachin State in Burma. Culturally and linguistically the Palaung can be divided into three main groups: the Shwe, the Rumai, and the Pale. The Shwe are also known as Golden Palaung or Ta-ang and the Pale as Silver Palaung or Di-ang. Ta-ang and Di-ang are the names used by the two groups of Palaung to identify themselves. There are approximately 600,000 Palaung in Burma and some 12,000 in China. Today there are also around a thousand Silver Palaung living in northern Thailand as refugees from the violence in Burma. The present study provides information on the Palaung in Burma, but focuses primarily on the Silver Palaung refugees in northern Thailand and their background and adaptation to their new environment.

These Silver Palaung or Di-ang refugees arrived in northern Thailand from Burma in 1984. They first settled just within Thailand at the village of No Lae on Doi Ang Khang in the Fang District of Chiang Mai Province. In fact, the border with Burma is on one edge of the village, where at present there is a small Thai military post. Later some of the Silver Palaung refugees left No Lae and eventually settled a few kilometers east of the town of Chiang Dao in order to further remove themselves from the violence and associated drug trafficking of the border area.

Our own involvement with the Palaung began in 1997 when one of us, Michael Howard, was engaged in writing a book on the textiles of the hill tribes of Burma (Howard 1999). One of the frustrations of

1.1. Pang Daeng Nai headman Kam-hieng

working on the book was the inability in many cases to talk to members of the various groups whose textiles were being studied. This was primarily because many of the areas in which they lived were closed to foreigners. Thus, he became quite excited when he came across a reference in a linguistic survey of Thailand to there being Silver Palaung in Thailand (Grimes 1992: 751). Despite having spent a great deal of time in northern Thailand, he had been unaware of the presence there of this group. Immediately he contacted a Ph.D. student under his supervision, Hideki Yoshikawa, who was in Chiang Mai at the time working on a research project on the Lue of Nan Province, and asked him to visit the Tribal Research Institute and see what he could find out. The graduate student was shown a brief report written in Thai by a staff member of the Tribal Research Institute (Shila 1993). He also made inquiries about where the Palaung were to be found. Eventually he discovered a local tour operator who knew of a Palaung village near Chiang Dao and offered to take us there. It was in this context that we first encountered what became a familiar refrain: "Don't you mean the Padaung, the Long-neck Karens?" It later turned out that many tour operators knew of the village; they simply did not identify it with the Palaung, but thought of it merely as a place where tourists were taken to be put on elephants for a ride in the countryside.

A short time later, accompanied by Hideki Yoshikawa, we made our first visit to Pang Daeng Nai, the Palaung village. On the way our guide assured us that there really was not much to see there, after asking us repeatedly if we were sure that we did not mean the Padaung. In fact, when we learned initially where the village was we were a little apprehensive since it was located in an area that over the years had been deluged with day-trippers and trekkers from Chiang Mai going on treks and elephant rides. The Lahu, Akha, and Karen villages in the area, frankly, were not very pleasant places to visit any longer. Nor was the forest in the area in very good condition. Nevertheless, we pressed on and what we discovered was quite a shock. Here, in the midst of degraded forest land and somewhat depressing hill tribe villages, was a surprisingly tidy hill tribe village with industrious women neatly dressed in traditional costumes busily weaving cloth on backstrap looms and repairing the thatch on their roofs. It was reminiscent of villages in the area decades ago, not the present. Our mood changed from one of apprehension to excited anticipation, which was soon rewarded as we began to meet the villagers.

The village of Pang Daeng Nai is where tourists from Chiang Mai commonly begin brief elephant rides in the area, and a small dormitory had been built for those few who wished to spend the night in the village to experience a bit of hill tribe culture. We parked next to this structure and were introduced to a neighboring family known to our guide. After talking to them for some time about weaving and dress and making arrangements for lunch, we set out to explore the village further. It was at this point that we were approached by a middle-aged man returning from the fields who engaged us in conversation. He turned out to be the village headman, Kam-hieng, and it did not take us very long to realize that we were talking to quite an exceptional person. In retrospect, it was this initial conversation with Kam-hieng more than anything else that made us decide to conduct further research among the Palaung. What began as a simple wish to find out a little more about Palaung dress quickly grew into a desire to find out much more about these people, their previous life in Burma, their flight to Thailand, and how they had adapted to life in northern Thailand.

The present study is intended primarily as an introduction to the Palaung in northern Thailand. We hope that it will serve to draw further attention to this group and, perhaps, generate greater understanding of the problems faced by them. The situation of the Palaung is also of more general interest for a variety of reasons. The story of their treatment by communists and others in Burma sheds light on this little-known segment of the warfare in Shan State and, more specifically, on communist recruitment activities. What has befallen them since coming to Thailand is relevant to our understanding of some of the fundamental developmental problems facing northern Thailand today, especially in regard to debates over the status of minority migrants and their use of highland lands.

PREVIOUS STUDIES OF THE PALAUNG

The literature on the ethnic minorities of Burma is very limited. Most of what exists consists of the writings of British colonial officers and Christian missionaries published during the early decades of the twentieth century. There are only a handful of monographs written by professional anthropologists. Anthropological research on the tribal minorities in Burma effectively came to a halt in 1962. Within even this very limited literature there is relatively little written about the Palaung. Moreover, what has been published concerning the Palaung is primarily about the Golden Palaung living in the northwestern part of Shan State. There is almost nothing written about the Silver Palaung in the southern and eastern parts of the state.

The earliest mention of the Palaung that we have found in English is by Michael Symes, in his *An Account of an Embassy to the Kingdom of Ava Sent by the Governor-General of India in the Year 1795.* Symes (1800: 273) mentions that on his way up the Irrawaddy River (currently spelled Ayeyarwady in Burma) to visit the Burman capital of Ava (near the present city of Mandalay) he stopped at a small village where "the inhabitants get their livelihood by selling Laepac, or pickled tea-leaf, of which the Birmans are extremely fond. The plant I was informed, grows at a place called Palong-miou, a district to the north-east of Ummerapora; it is very inferior to the tea produced in China, and is seldom used but as a pickle." It is this pickled tea, popular among lowland Burmans, for which the Palaung are still best known within Burma.

A little more information is provided in Henry Yule's (1858) account of his mission to the Court of Ava in 1855. Like Symes, Yule did not visit the Palaung himself and bases what he has to say about them on information gathered by others. In a footnote relating to the Palaung selling fermented tea to the Burmese, he cites Colonel Hannay, who describes the Palaung "as having the character of being an industrious and hospitable race, good dyers, carpenters, and blacksmiths . . . " (Yule 1858: 149). Yule later describes the Palaung living in the hills "east of Bamo and Koungtoun" as the "breeches-wearing Paloungs, peaceably growing tea for pickling" (275). He also comments that "the Paloungs

Shan State and northwestern Thailand

(called also Paloo) are said to resemble the Shan and to be of Shan kindred," but he expresses his doubt about this and suggests that they might be a Karen tribe (295). The Karen at this time were one of the better-known minorities to the British, who still had only a vague idea about the various minority groups living in Shan State.

In his survey of materials written about the British annexation of Shan State in the 1880s, Sao Saimong Mangrai (1965) does not mention the Palaung directly, but does have a few references to the ruler (known as *chaofa* or *sawbwa*) of Tawngpeng at the time. Tawngpeng was a largely Palaung area in northwestern Shan State (and located northeast of Mandalay) which was occupied primarily by Golden Palaung. Burma Foreign Department documents from 1886 portray the chaofa as "living peacefully since his appointment by King Mindon in 1877. . . in the fastness of his tea mountains, . . . little affected by internecine strife around his State" and generally trying to avoid being seen as taking sides in the conflict (Mangrai 1965: 127). Reports relating to British troop movements in early 1888 note that villagers in Tawngpeng and in the capital of Namhsan (including the chaofa) fled into the hills in advance of the British column moving through the state and that the chaofa "could not be induced" to meet with the British commander despite numerous entreaties (155). There is no mention of the Palaung in Mangrai's discussions concerning Keng Tung State.

The first serious effort to describe the Palaung is Scott and Hardiman's entry on the "Rumai or Palaungs" in volume one of their *Gazetteer of Upper Burma and the Shan States* (1900: 483–93), which begins with the comment that: "This race is so quiet and peaceable that it has not been much studied." They go on to note that "no one as yet has made a study of their language, and all that is known is derived through Burmese or Shan and has inevitably been colored in the process" (486). They cautiously suggest that the Rumai and Palaung have a linguistic connection with the Wa and possibly with other hill-dwelling Mon-Khmer speaking peoples such as the Stieng (who live along the border of Cambodia and Vietnam). At the same time they reject a connection with the Mon, which had been suggested by Professor Forchhammer. The study of Southeast Asian languages was

1.2. "Palaungs." From Scott (1921), facing p. 132.

in its infancy at this time, but a general picture of the Mon-Khmer languages was beginning to emerge and on the basis of geographical distance and cultural differences it is easy to understand why Scott and Hardiman had difficulty in seeing a relationship between the Palaung and the Mon.

Their account is primarily about the Golden Palaung of Tawngpeng, but they do have a few comments about other Palaung as well. In discussing the location of the Palaung, Scott and Hardiman (1900: 493) make a reference to the Palaung in Keng Tung State, who are presumably Silver Palaung. They quote from an account by Mr. Stirling, who states that "there are very few villages of this race in Kengtung State. All that are known have been here for many years, but they believe their forefathers came from Tawngpeng." This agrees in broad terms with current oral history accounts.

Scott and Hardiman (1900: I: 486) state that "there is a vague general division into Palaungs and Pales which has a basis in distinction of dress and dialect, but is Burmese rather than national." They then place the Pale to the west of the Palaung and state that the Palaung live at higher elevations and primarily grow tea, while the Pale live at lower levels and tend to grow more rice than tea. They also point to administrative divisions among the Palaung and to those based on what is referred to as clanship: "the *Kadu* round Nam Hsan, the capital; the *Padwè* round Man Loi and Kong Hsa; the *Teao Rai* round Nam Lin; the *Kawn Gyawn* round Tawng Ma and Tawng Mè; the *Kawn Lè*, who seem to correspond to the Pale." They note that in Rumai the term Pale "seems to mean 'the tribe of the west.'" Most of their description is devoted to the Golden Palaung and, to a lesser extent, to the Rumai. The only specific reference to the Pale is about marriage customs and about how marriage arrangements differ between the two groups (490).

Additional information on the Palaung based on first hand accounts, but not long-term systematic fieldwork, appears a short time later in two reports. The first is Cecil Lowis's brief account of the Palaung in the Hsipaw and Tawngpeng area. Published in 1906, it is the first volume of the Ethnographical Survey of India series of monographs devoted to Burma. The second one is A. A. Cameron's (1912) report on the Palaung and Rumai of the Kodaung Hill Tracts in Momeik

(Muang Mit) State published in the 1911 census of India. Cameron thus covers Palaung living to the north of those described by Lowis. Combined, these reports give us an outline of the social organization, economic activities, and religious beliefs of the Golden Palaung and Rumai in the northwestern part of Shan State. Cameron's report is especially useful in providing a picture of Palaung and Rumai life in Muang Mit State rather than Tawngpeng. The Palaung in this area, prior to the establishment of British rule, although nominally under the Shan chaofa of Muang Mit, are reported by Cameron (1912: 33–4) to have been paying tribute to the Jingpho in order to ward off their attacks.

1.3. "Group of girls." From Milne (1924), facing p. 116.

Scott's handbook of Burma, first published in 1911, with a third updated edition published in 1921, includes the Palaung among the "Wa-Rumai Clans" who are treated along with the Mon or Talaing as part of the "Môn-Hkmêr Sub-family" (1921: 62). There is a brief section devoted to the "Rumai, or Palaungs" (131–3). They are said to have their headquarters in Tawngpeng and also to be found in "the adjacent Kodaung tract" and in "scattered villages" throughout the Shan states (131). The section describes their dress and refers to their near monopoly on the production of pickled tea. Scott remarks that "as a race they are peaceable and industrious, but have a reputation of being hypocritical, and they are certainly rough and uncouth" (133). One assumes that the latter is in comparison with the Shan. Among the photos in the handbook is one of the sawbwa of Tawngpeng and his wives (facing p. 115) and another of a Palaung man and two women in front of what appears to be a rough temporary shelter without reference to the location (facing p. 132).

The first and only person to carry out prolonged and systematic fieldwork among the Palaung was Leslie Milne. She first mentions the Palaung in her well known 1910 book on the Shan, *Shans at Home*. In this book she briefly describes Palaung dress, tea growing, being Buddhists, and avoidance of "intoxicating liquors," and remarks that: "Before the British occupation, when Shans and Kachins were constantly fighting, the Palaungs lived in peace with their fierce neighbors, paying tribute to them" (Milne 1910: 135).

Later her attention turned to studying the Palaung in more detail. Two main publications emerged from this work, the first was *An Elementary Palaung Grammar*, published in 1921, and the second was a comprehensive ethnography on the Palaung of Tawngpeng State, *The Home of an Eastern Clan*, published in 1924. *The Home of an Eastern Clan* is the only detailed ethnographic account of the Palaung that has been written to date. It has not been widely read and surveys of literature on minorities in Burma tend to pay it scant attention. Yet it is a very well-written and reasoned book that contains an impressive amount of information on the Palaung and should be seen as an important contribution to the ethnographic literature of Burma.

In the introduction to *The Home of an Eastern Clan,* Milne (1924: 4) notes that "in the autumn of 1911, when I was in Mandalay, I met the ruling Chief of Tawngpeng, who gave me an invitation to go up to his country." Off and on over the next couple of years she resided in Namhsan and traveled about Tawngpeng State studying the language (see Milne 1921) and life of the Golden Palaung.

Milne believed that the ancestors of the Palaung were driven by various invaders, such as the Shan, "to the tops of the hills" where they eventually took up the cultivation of tea (1924: 17). She comments that, although they occasionally fought among themselves over political offices, "on the whole, they have been a peaceful agricultural people" who generally did not take part in the fighting involving other groups, but sold tea to all sides: "Secure in their hill-tops, they were hardly touched by the waves of battle that surged to and fro in the valleys below." She does note, however, that this situation did tend to cut them off from one another: "In this way the different Palaung clans, and even the different groups of the same clan, separated from one another . . . , developed different dialects, different customs, and, as regards the women, different dress" (18). In regard to the Burman division of the Palaung into Palaung and Pale, she remarks that "it is difficult to know why some clans were called by them Palaungs and some Palês," except that "Palaungs do not generally wear cane girdles as do the Palês" (18, fn. 2). She has little more to say specifically about the Pale (Silver Palaung), but does include a couple of relevant photos: one of a "Palê girl spinning" (facing p. 138) and one of a Rumai woman (facing p. 370) who is dressed in a similar fashion as the Pale (Silver Palaung). While Milne's monograph provides a wealth of data on the Palaung, as she notes herself, care must be taken in making generalizations about Palaung outside of the Tawngpeng area based on her account.

No additional substantive fieldwork has been conducted among the Palaung in Burma since Milne carried out her study prior to the First World War. In recent decades, those seeking information on the Palaung generally have turned to the section on them in Lebar, Hickey, and Musgrave's survey volume, *Ethnic Groups of Mainland Southeast Asia,* published by the Human Relations Area Files in 1964 (121–6). This account provides a useful summary of the earlier works by Cameron, Lowis, Milne, Scott, and others without adding any new information. There are also a few references to the Palaung in Leach's (1954) influential *Political Systems of Highland Burma*. Leach himself did not conduct fieldwork among the Palaung and relies on these same earlier sources for most of his data.

Although Shan State has attracted a good deal of attention since the 1960s because of its role in the international narcotics trade and various military conflicts between insurgents associated with the communists and minority groups and the central government, published works on these topics generally have ignored the Palaung. The Palaung have had only a minor role in the drama and it has primarily been that of victim rather than active participant. Martin Smith's (1991) monumental work on the ethnic insurgencies in Burma has a handful of brief references to the Palaung. These are mainly regarding the relatively small Palaung State Liberation Organization/Party, based in Tawngpeng. Besides noting its existence and varying alliances, however, Smith's work gives us very little detailed information on this organization and how it relates to Palaung society as a whole. Nevertheless, and despite not mentioning the Silver Palaung at all, Smith's and other such works are of relevance to the present study in that they provide useful background material concerning the reasons why the Silver Palaung now living in Thailand fled from Shan State.

The most recent source on the Palaung in Burma is Richard Diran's book, *The Vanishing Tribes of Burma* (1997). This is essentially a picture book and it contains numerous mistakes in the text, but the photos are often useful. There is a brief chapter on the Palaung (72–5) that provides several photos of what he calls Pale (or Silver Palaung) from Pin Ne Bang near Kalaw in southwestern Shan State and Shwe Palaung (also known as Golden Palaung) in the Keng Tung area in eastern Shan State. Some of his statements are open to question and it is possible that those he identifies as Golden Palaung near Keng Tung are in fact Silver Palaung. Certainly the blouse that he identifies (lower right, p. 73) as typically Golden Palaung is of a type commonly worn by the Silver Palaung (see the discussion on dress in chapter 3 of the present work).

The author relied on Burmese guides for his information, and tourist guides in Burma, as in most countries, often are not particularly knowledgeable about minority groups and the information that they disseminate about them is commonly inaccurate.

Toward the end of Diran's book there are a few paragraphs on the Palaung based on written material available in England (1997: 209–10) and two black and white archival photos of Palaung: one from 1905 of Palaung in Lawsawk State and another from the 1920s. The latter (on p. 208) is from the James Henry Green Collection, a valuable and little-used resource of ethnographic material on the tribal people of Burma. Again, there are some inaccuracies in the data presented. Thus, it is stated that "the Palaungs call themselves Ta-ang," whereas the name Ta-ang refers to a group of Palaung, the Shwe or Golden Palaung, and not the Palaung as a whole.

Although we will discuss the matter at greater length in chapter 3, mention should also be made of the relevant literature on Palaung dress. As we note there, unfortunately, the museum catalogues that discuss textiles from Shan State do not include Palaung material. However, Michael Howard's *Textiles of the Hill Tribes of Burma* (1999), does include several Palaung pieces from the collection of the Bankfield Museum.

In regard to the Palaung in Thailand, they have been almost completely ignored in publications on minorities in northern Thailand. One reason for this is that the major surveys of hill tribes in northern Thailand were written largely before the arrival of the Palaung in 1984. However, this does not entirely explain why they have been so widely ignored since then. McKinnon and Bhruksasri's edited volume, *Highlanders of Thailand* (1983), was published before the Palaung came to Thailand. Anthony Walker's edited volume, *The Highland Heritage* (1992: 35–43), contains a survey of Mon-Khmer peoples in northern Thailand, but makes no specific reference to the Palaung in Thailand.

The only previously published account of the Palaung in northern Thailand is the one to which we referred earlier by Sarapi Shila, her 1993 report for the Tribal Research Institute. This brief report reviews the history of the Palaung in Burma, their recent problems in Burma and along the Thai border, and their settlement history in Thailand. It also provides a brief survey of certain aspects of their material culture, social organization, and religious beliefs and practices. Short as it is and despite its being based on only a limited period of research, Shila's report is a very good introduction to the Palaung in Thailand.

The Palaung are not the only Mon-Khmer speaking people in northern Thailand. Other groups that have been resident in northern Thailand for some time include the Khmuic speaking Khmu and Htin (also known as T'in or Mal) and the Palaungic speaking Lua (or Lawa). McKinnon and Bhruksasri (1983: 17) estimated that there were 36,963 Mon-Khmer speakers in northern Thailand belonging to these groups around 1970. The Lua language is the one of these most closely linked to Palaung (see Thomas and Headley 1970) and there is thus a potential for comparative studies of the two groups. Peter Kunstadter and Hans Kauffmann have published extensively on the Lua in Thailand (see Kunstadter's chapter in McKinnon and Bhruksasri 1983).

THE PRESENT STUDY

The majority of our fieldwork for the present study was conducted in Pang Daeng Nai, east of the small town of Chiang Dao. We also made a visit to the Palaung village of No Lae at Doi Ang Khang in late 1998, and Michael Howard visited two Palaung communities near Kalaw in Burma in early 1999. In addition to the published sources described above, we have also collected written materials from newspapers and elsewhere relating to problems of the Palaung with Thai authorities.

The remainder of our study is divided into five chapters. The following chapter, chapter 2, is an overview of Palaung society and history in Burma based on published sources and fieldwork near Kalaw. Chapter 2 begins with linguistic and demographic background and includes sections on settlement patterns and economic activities, life cycle, social and political organization, and religious beliefs and practices. Chapter 3 focuses on Palaung dress and how it relates to their identity. The chapter includes four sections: a comparative look at the dress of neighboring Mon-Khmer speaking peoples, a review of previous descriptions of Palaung dress, a section on sub-group differences in dress, and a section on the dress of the Silver Palaung. Chapter 4 discusses the flight from Burma by the Silver Palaung now living at Doi Ang Khan and Pang Daeng. Chapter 5 looks at life in the different Palaung communities in northern Thailand (primarily Pang Daeng and No Lae), while chapter 6 discusses recent conflicts in which they have become embroiled, relating to their official status as migrants and land issues.

CHAPTER 2

THE PALAUNG IN BURMA

To place the Palaung in context, it is first necessary to describe how their language fits into the broader linguistic picture in Southeast Asia and neighboring regions of China and India. The languages spoken by the Palaung belong to the Austro-Asiatic stock of languages, which in turn are placed by some linguists in a super-stock known as Austric that also includes the Austro-Tai stock (see Reid 1993). Austric speakers initially lived along the Yangtze River with the Austro-Asiatic languages developing in the upper reaches of the river and the Austro-Tai languages developing in the lower region nearer to the sea some 7,000 to 8,500 years ago. Rice cultivation played a central role in the lives of these people.

The Austro-Asiatic languages are thought to have been introduced into mainland Southeast Asia from southern China at least 4,000 years ago (see Diffloth 1991). Speakers of early Austro-Asiatic languages moved from the upper Yangtze River south into Yunnan. From there they moved into areas in northern mainland Southeast Asia adjacent to the Chinese border and then moved south and west, following the main rivers: the Mekong, Irrawaddy, and Brahmaputra. There are approximately 150 languages in the Austro-Asiatic stock. These languages are divided into two families: Mon-Khmer and Munda. Munda languages are spoken today in northern India. Mon-Khmer languages are spoken throughout mainland Southeast Asia as well as in northern India. The latter are divided into six branches: Northern Mon-Khmer, Monic, Eastern Mon-Khmer, Vietic, Aslian, and Nicobarese.

THE PALAUNG IN MYANMAR

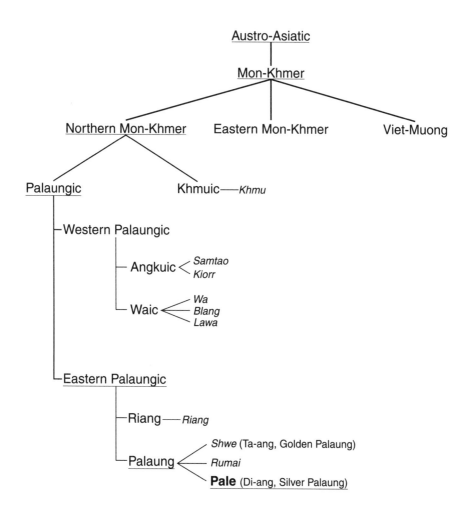

Linguistic relationships of Palaung languages

Munda and Mon-Khmer languages spoken in India are associated with what is called the Eastern Neolithic Culture that emerged in eastern India between 1500 BC and 1000 BC (see Dani 1960).

Sometime between 2000 BC and 1000 BC early Mon-Khmer speaking peoples settled in Burma, probably along its main river systems. While Burma was inhabited prior to the arrival of Mon-Khmer speaking peoples, among the contemporary peoples of Burma the Mon-Khmer may be seen as the indigenous population, although not necessarily the Palaung themselves. The Mon-Khmer family is represented in Burma by languages belonging to the Monic and Northern Mon-Khmer branches. The main Monic language is Mon. Mon was once spoken extensively in the lowlands of central Thailand and lower Burma and is associated with the Indian-influenced Dvaravati period in Thailand and the state of Pegu (or Bago) in Burma (these lasting from the sixth century to the eleventh century AD). The Northern Mon-Khmer languages stretch from northwestern Vietnam to northern India and are linked with upland peoples who did not form states.

The Northern Mon-Khmer languages are divided into four sub-branches: Mang, Khasian, Khmuic, and Palaungic. The Mang sub-branch is located farthest to the east along the border of China and Vietnam and the Khasian sub-branch farthest to the west in India and Bangladesh. Khmuic speakers live in adjacent areas of northwestern Vietnam, southern China, northern Thailand, and northeastern Burma. Khmu is the most widely spoken Khmuic language. Most Khmu speakers live in Laos, but a small number also live in northeastern Burma.

People speaking the Palaungic languages are located in southwestern Yunnan (mainly in Dehong), Burma's Shan State and southern Kachin State, and northern Thailand. The Palaungic sub-branch is divided into an eastern group and a western group. The Western Palaungic group includes what are known as Waic and Angkuic languages. These are spoken in southwestern Yunnan and northeastern Burma. The Waic languages are associated primarily with the Wa (or Vo) in Burma and China, made famous by their headhunting practices and their more recent association with the Communist Party of Burma and heroin trafficking in Burma, and the Lawa (or Lua) of China and northern Thailand.

The Eastern Palaungic languages include Pale, Rumai, and Shwe (which are closely related to one another) as well as Riang (sometimes known as Black Karen), Yinchia (also known as Striped Karen or Black Riang), and Danau. Pale speakers are also called Di-ang, Ngwe Palaung, or Silver Palaung. Shwe speakers are also known as Ta-ang or Golden Palaung.

It is difficult to determine precisely how long the Palaung have lived in what is now Burma. As will be discussed in more detail later in the chapter, their legends have them living first near the present town of Namh Kam, located in Burma just across the border from the Chinese town of Ruili. After the region where they were living was conquered by the Chinese, according to Palaung chronicles they migrated to the area around the present town of Namhsan, to the north of Hsipaw. This area has remained the center of Palaung settlement, but over the years, as told in various oral histories, the Palaung scattered from Namhsan and its vicinity throughout Shan State. In addition, other Palaung (especially Rumai) migrated south from the China-Burma border area more recently.

There are between 200,000 and 300,000 Silver Palaung, around 150,000 Golden Palaung, and about 135,000 Rumai living in Burma, primarily in Shan State. In Shan State they are to be found scattered over an area stretching from the vicinity of Namh Kam, near the Chinese border in the north, to Muang Mit and Namhsan to the west, to the hills around Kalaw in the southwest, and in the hills south of Keng Tung toward the Thai border in the east. Some Golden Palaung also live in southeastern Kachin State. The Silver Palaung live primarily around Kalaw as well as to the south of Keng Tung. The Golden Palaung live mainly in the former Shan state of Tawngpeng (also known as Taungbaing) which has its capital at Namhsan. The Rumai live mostly to the north of Tawngpeng. There are also small numbers of Palaung living in lowland towns and cities, including Rangoon and Mandalay.

The pattern of migration and settlement of the Silver Palaung throughout eastern and southern Shan State is for a group first to settle on a mountain slope in a single community and gradually to found a number of related villages in the vicinity. Silver Palaung oral history says that they originally lived in Namhsan area. Around two hundred years ago (the date is not precise), some Silver Palaung moved to the Keng Tung area. A story is told among Silver Palaung today that the ruler of Namhsan at this time wanted to levy a tax on the people. It was to be a tax per room, but the ancestors of the Silver Palaung mistakenly believed that he was demanding that they fill a room with money and fled east to the area around Keng Tung rather than pay this heavy tax. Later, groups of these Silver Palaung migrated to the south and west of Keng Tung as well. Among these was a group that settled around Loi Lae in the 1930s. The Silver Palaung now living in Thailand come from this group. The Silver Palaung living near Kalaw moved there during the late nineteenth and early twentieth centuries. One informant's grandfather who was born in the village of Nyaung Gone (near Kalaw) in 1933 was among those who founded the first village in this area.

There are a small number of Palaung in China, where they are classified as members of an officially recognized nationality known as De'ang. Formerly this nationality was named Benglong by the Chinese. There are around 16,000 people classified as De'ang living in the Dehong region in western Yunnan Province (Shanghai Theatrical College 1986: 216), adjacent to the town of Namh Kam in Burma. In this part of Dehong, Tai live at the lower elevations and Wa and Lisu live around and above the De'ang/Palaung in the hills. The De'ang nationality includes an estimated 2,000 Golden Palaung (Ta-ang Palaung), 5,000 Silver Palaung (Di-ang Palaung), and about 2,000 Rumai (Grimes 1999).

It appears that there was some migration of Palaung from China to British Burma in the late nineteenth and early twentieth centuries as a result of the instability in Yunnan at the time, in contrast to the more stable situation in the British territory. Milne notes that "when I was in Yün-nan, I met many Palaungs of the Rumai clan, who told me that life was so uncertain under Chinese rule that they thought of migrating to British territory. This may account for the increase of their numbers in the Northern Shan States."

Other than language, it is difficult to tell from the existing literature precisely how the Golden Palaung, Silver Palaung, and Rumai differ culturally. Female dress is one other difference that is widely commented on, although no comprehensive study of Palaung dress has yet been made. (We will discuss dress at greater length in chapter 3.) Palaung men dress in the same manner as other men in the region. In general, Golden Palaung and Silver Palaung women dress differently. This can readily be seen in their skirts and type of headcloth. Also, as was noted by Milne, Silver Palaung women wear rattan hoops and Golden Palaung women do not. Silver Palaung and Rumai women, however, dress much more alike (both wear rattan hoops). It is worth noting that the dress of women from all three groups differs in easily identifiable ways from that of other ethnolinguistic groups living around them.

The most important neighbors of the Palaung in Burma are the Tai-speaking Shan (or Tai Yai) and the Jingpho (or Kachin). The Shan moved into the valleys of the Shan Plateau from the east and established small principalities throughout the region between the seventh and twelfth centuries and became the most important political and cultural presence in what is now Shan State. The Jingpho arrived later, invading northern Burma and in the process cutting off the Tai living to the west of the Shan Plateau from those in Shan State and driving many Palaung and others south from what is now Kachin State. Also living around and above (at higher altitudes) the Silver Palaung are members of other ethnolinguistic groups. These include the Pa-o Karen in the area east of Kalaw and Lahu (or Muhso) in Keng Tung State. Elsewhere there are Lisu living near the Palaung as well.

The Shan, as rulers of the states that comprised the area now included in Shan State and the dominant culture in the area, exerted an especially strong influence on the Palaung. Milne (1924: 23) remarks that the Palaung "are becoming absorbed by the Shans of the Southern Shan States." Leach (1954: 47) notes that "Tai and Jinghpaw speaking groups have constantly tended to assimilate their Naga, Maru and Palaung speaking neighbors." More specifically, he comments that "Shans and Palaungs intermarry, and in general culture the tea-raising Palaung are far closer to the Shans than any of the other hill peoples of the area. Moreover Palaung and Shan are members of a common political system" (49). He reports that the situation is different to the north of Tawngpeng where Palaung settlements are interspersed between Jingpho settlements and that intermarriage between Palaung and Jingpho is negligible (57).

For the Silver Palaung living to the south and east of the Golden Palaung and Rumai, it has been the Shan and not the Jingpho who have had the most influence. Many Silver Palaung and other Palaung have spoken Shan as a second language apparently for quite some time. The Silver Palaung have been Buddhists for several centuries and the version practiced by them is largely of the Shan variety. Politically they were integrated into Shan principalities, although some degree of local autonomy prevailed.

The Burmese also have exerted influence on the Palaung for many centuries, although mainly more indirectly than the Shan and Jingpho. Milne (1924: 23) does note, however, that the Palaung are "becoming absorbed . . . by the Burmans of Katha" in Kachin State. Burmese kings periodically included Palaung territories within their domain, collecting tribute from them and sometimes appointing local rulers. This was especially true after King Alaung-hpaya (who ruled from 1752 to 1760) asserted Burmese suzerainty over many of the Shan principalities. The lowland Burmese also have been a major market for the Palaung's pickled tea. While Buddhism appears to have first been introduced to the Palaung by the Shan, the Burmese variant of Buddhism was also adopted by some Palaung.

The sections below provide a summary of Palaung settlement patterns, economic life, the life cycle, social and political organization, and religious beliefs and practices in Burma based mainly on existing ethnographic literature and, to a lesser extent, on fieldwork near Kalaw. Thus, it is largely a picture of Palaung life in the early twentieth century rather than of the contemporary situation in Burma.

SETTLEMENT PATTERNS AND ECONOMIC ACTIVITIES

The Palaung live in a region featuring narrow upland valleys interspersed between mountains reaching elevations of up to 2,000 meters. In general, the Golden Palaung live at higher elevations than the Silver Palaung. The Palaung live in compact villages located along ridges or on top of hills. Cameron (1912: 9) reports that in Muang

2.1. "House and front verandah where basket-making is in progress." From Milne (1924), facing p. 193.

Mit, villages range in size from two to fifty houses with an average of about ten houses. Between three and six families live in these houses. Further south, in Tawngpeng, Milne (1924: 179) describes the houses as having only one or two families on average. Silver Palaung villages near Kalaw vary in size, with populations ranging from a couple of hundred to several hundred people. Nyaung Gone, for example, has about 600 people. In the past, Silver Palaung often lived in multiple-family houses (long houses), but these have become fairly rare in recent years. In the Kalaw area, for example, there is only one such house remaining today.

Traditional Palaung houses are raised on wooden posts from one to four meters off the ground. The height varies according to the slope of the land. The houses range in length from ten to twenty meters and are sometimes longer. While wealthier Palaung construct their houses out of wooden planks, most houses are made largely out of bamboo. The roofs are made of thatch and extend almost to the floor. Open verandahs are used as entrances and for kitchen activities. In the case of multiple family houses, there are two styles. In those described by Cameron in Muang Mit each family dwelling unit in a multiple-family house has a separate verandah. Within the house there are separate rooms for sleeping and storage. There are fireplaces within the houses, but few other furnishings. The multiple-family house near Kalaw has only a single entrance and verandah at one end. Within the house one half of the house is a long open space with baskets for storage and other goods scattered about on the floor. The other half contains individual family units. These consist of two parts: one part is a closed area with a doorway where the family sleeps and the other part is open on a raised platform that includes the family cooking hearth.

Prior to British rule, settlements were surrounded by stockades which were locked at night. At one end of larger villages or sometimes at their center is a Buddhist monastery, a house of Buddhist images, a rest house, and often a market area. Villages also usually have one or more shrines for guardian spirits (see photo facing p. 344 in Milne 1924). Silver Palaung villages always have a shrine for guardian spirits located just outside of the village (called a *jaw moeng* or *chao moeng*) and a shrine, known as the village heart, the *huja rawl,* located within the village (usually more or less at its center). There is also a graveyard (*parero*) located outside of the village.

Living at higher elevations, the Golden Palaung traditionally grew less rice than the Silver Palaung. Swidden rice growing is practiced at higher elevations, while irrigated rice is grown at lower levels. Among the other crops grown in swidden fields are tea, beans, peas, sesame, corn, tobacco, hemp, yams, and chilies. There are also household gardens and, in some areas, fruit trees. The villages near Kalaw grow a variety of crops. These include rice (including a little sticky rice), sesame,

2.2. "Village on the spur of a hill." From Milne (1924), facing p. 200.

corn, tea (to be dried and pickled), a variety of vegetables, and flowers for sale at the Kalaw market.

It is their tea, especially pickled tea, for which the Palaung are best known. Scott and Hardiman (1900: 491–2) provide a legend about the introduction of tea by "the great lord Yamadi-kyè-thu" in the early sixteenth century. The story tells of how the great lord visited a hill known as "Loi-seng" (Milne spells it "Lawi-seng") near Tawngpeng. The white elephant on which he was riding knelt before the hill "indicating the presence of some relic of Buddha" and when some bones were found he declared the site a place of worship. He then gave two Pa-o Karen

2.3. "Village houses with spirit-shrine" [probably a village heart or *huja rawl*]. From Milne (1924), facing p. 344.

hunters a seed which he had found in a dead bird to plant. The unfortunate hunters held out only one hand to receive the seed and not two "as etiquette and respect demanded" and the great lord told them that they could have become rich, but because of this slight they would be poor. From this seed, according to the legend, came the first tea tree in the area, which later became an object of worship by the Palaung. Milne (1924, facing p. 226) provides a photo of the tree.

Milne (1924: 226–38) gives a detailed description of Palaung tea cultivation and preparation of pickled tea. Because of its importance economically to the Palaung and its association with them, below we quote Milne's description of pickled tea pits and pickled tea preparation:

> For preparation of the pickled tea, holes in the shape of a well are dug in the ground; they are from six to twelve feet deep and vary in width. They also vary in the way in which they are prepared for the tea, as different families have different methods. One of these pits I examined: it measured two yards in diameter. About two feet from the bottom was fixed a floor of planks roughly fastened together, allowing a space for the water to drain away from the tea leaves resting upon it. The sides of some of the pits are lined with bamboos, and also with banana leaves, so that the earth cannot touch the tea. In other pits the lining is of brick, made smooth with mortar, and there is no false bottom. These pits often have an inner lining of the leaves of the *taungsin*. Each pit and the surrounding ground is protected from rain by a thatched roof, supported on poles. Sometimes two or more pits are dug side by side, on level ground if possible, and one roof covers all. A channel is dug so that water dripping from the roof may not run down into the pit or pits. If a tea garden is small, there may be only one pit in it; if large, there may be a good many.
>
> The sides of a pit having been lined, a wooden press is brought in sections to the hole. The part that rests upon the tea leaves and presses them down is composed of three loose boards of thick and heavy wood, which when laid in position roughly fit the hole. These pieces are not joined together, as at first the tea does not fill up the pit, and it is easier to remove the pieces separately when more tea is added than if they were

joined together. The middle board slightly overlaps the edges of the other two. The boards are removed by a man who descends by means of a bamboo ladder, or by a single large bamboo which has notches cut here and there to give a foothold. When the press is in position, an upright pole rests on the middle board, and it projects from the top of the pit. Across the top of this pole is placed a heavy piece of wood, which passes through two upright pieces of wood fixed firmly in the ground, two feet or more on either side of the pit; this cross-piece is weighted at the ends and sometimes in the middle with large stones. When the day's picking has been steamed, rolled and weighed, the press is removed, and the leaves are thrown into the pit; the press is immediately placed in position again.

The owner of the tea garden sometimes sells the whole of the pit after three months' time. If, however, he has not sold it by July or August, he opens the pit and sprinkles water on the leaves; it depends on the dryness or wetness of the season when the pickling is done, how much water must be added; sometimes the contents of only one bamboo joint is used, sometimes more water is required. Pickled tea may be eaten after it has been one month in the pit, but when it has been kept for several months, it is considered to be of much better quality and it fetches a higher price . . .

Tea cultivation by the Palaung beyond Tawngpeng appears to have been a relatively recent innovation and even in the case of Tawngpeng the evidence suggests that large-scale commercial production, as reported by Milne (1924: 230) in the early twentieth century, was a new development associated with economic changes under British rule. Scott (1921: 269–70) indicates that there were no large tea plantations even in the Tawngpeng area in the 1890s and Cameron (1912: 26) reports that the Rumai of Muang Mit were only just starting to grow tea. By the time of Milne's research, however, it was indeed a large industry in Tawngpeng, involving both large and small plantations and paid labor (such laborers often being from less well off groups such as the Lisu). Writing from the perspective of a few decades later, Leach (1954: 26) remarks in regard to the Palaung of Tawngpeng that,

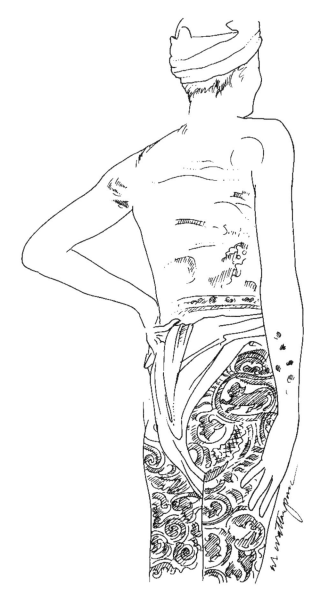

2.4. Palaung man showing tattoos. Drawing based on a photograph in Milne (1924), facing p. 268.

although they are a hill people, they "manage to maintain Shan standards of life by means of their long established trade in tea." In addition to growing and processing tea, the Palaung also engaged in transporting it for sale to the Shan and Burmese.

The Palaung are predominantly vegetarians and their diet consists mainly of rice with stews or curries of cultivated or wild plants (see Cameron 1912: 27–8; Lowis 1906: 14; and Milne 1924: 192–3). Meat and other animal products are eaten on occasion, primarily by men. Milne (1924: 195) notes that in addition to dogs and cats, the Palaung never eat frogs, but that the Shan do and that "when a Palaung is angry with a Shan, he sometimes calls him a 'frog-eater' as a mark of contempt." Although the Palaung raise animals, they do not raise them for slaughter, but to be used as beasts of burden or for sale to non-Palaung. Cameron (1912: 26) alone mentions Palaung raising pigs. Other animals mentioned include sheep, goats, ducks, chickens and roosters, buffalo, cattle, and horses. For the most part, the Palaung traditionally obtained meat from Chinese butchers or from neighboring Jingpho, Lahu or Lisu who have slaughtered animals for ceremonies. Preserved fish are obtained on occasion from Burmese. They also will eat the meat of animals killed by predators. The Palaung rarely eat eggs and do not consume milk products.

Industrial arts among the Palaung are relatively limited and are intended only for domestic use (weaving and dress will be discussed at greater length in chapter 3). They make relatively simple baskets, but also often purchase them. Clothing and utilitarian bags are often made from cloth obtained from the Shan, although some cloth is woven and women embroider patterns on some of the cloth they obtain from others. There are reported to be a few Palaung silversmiths, but most jewelry is obtained from the Shan. Other metal objects (e.g., plowshares) are obtained from the Chinese or others, although Palaung blacksmiths do make repairs. Work on the larger Buddhist religious structures is done mainly by Burmese craftsmen.

To purchase the items discussed above the Palaung trade pickled and dried tea, livestock (especially horses), and other agricultural products (such as beans). The Palaung themselves work as traders and their villages are also visited by Shan, Chinese, Burmese, and Indian itinerant

2.5. Young girl. Drawing based on photograph of "Group of girls" in
Milne (1924), facing p. 116.

traders. In addition to small village markets, there are also larger markets in the main towns in the Palaung area, and various writers note that Palaung traders also take goods to Mandalay and other lowland towns. Among the other commercial goods obtained by the Palaung are kerosene, lacquerware, religious objects, betel nut, and various food items (such as preserved fish, sugar, salt, and biscuits).

While Cameron (1912: 36–7) reports that betel nut is not grown in Muang Mit, Milne (1924: 192) comments that the Palaung are avid consumers of it. Such apparent inconsistencies may reflect local differences or inaccuracies in the reports. There are differing reports concerning consumption of alcohol as well. Lowis (1906: 14) states that it is rarely drunk, whereas Cameron (1912: 27) reports that it is present at most festivals. In this case, both could be true if one is led to understand that alcohol consumption takes place mainly at festivals.

The role of opium among the Palaung in the past is difficult to assess as it is rarely mentioned in the literature. Cameron (1912: 26–7) states that the Palaung do not cultivate opium. It is likely, however, that some opium cultivation took place for tribute payment to Shan rulers. Much of the opium cultivation that is encountered among the Palaung in Burma today, however, is associated with the coercive practices of the KMT forces starting in the 1950s (to be discussed in the next chapter).

THE LIFE CYCLE

A good deal of Milne's (1924) monograph is devoted to describing in some detail the life cycle among the Palaung of Tawnpeng. There are occasional references to differences found among other Palaung.

A newly born child and its mother remain indoors near the fire in the inner room until the child is one month old. The fire is fed wood that the father has collected prior to the birth. The child is then taken to the temple and offerings are placed before Buddha and given to monks. Around this time, without an accompanying ceremony, the child is also given a personal name which is related to which day of the week it was born; e.g., Nan Yon is Wednesday, so a person born on

2.6. Village elder. Drawing based on a photograph in Milne (1924), facing p. 164.

Wednesday would be named Yon. At the time of Milne's study, the Palaung did not use surnames. Later surnames were adopted and a person took his or her father's surname. Upon marriage a woman would take her husband's family name. Elderly widowed women who practice Buddhist precepts and stay in the temple take religious names.

The Palaung practice string-tying rites for young children around the age of three months similar to those of the Tai and other neighboring groups. As Milne (1924: 27–8, 418) notes, however, the precise practice varies among different groups of Palaung in regards to what is tied (wrists, neck, waist, or ankles) and the colors of the string (white or red apparently being the most common colors, with silver sometimes replacing cord).

Prior to marriage, the conduct of boys and girls is supervised by an elderly man and woman referred to by Milne (1924: 60) as "*pak-ke dang*" or great pak-ke. The office is held for life and the pak-ke are chosen by the chief in consultation with the population at large. In Namhsan at least there are also assistant pak-ke known as "*pak-ke taw*" or pak-ka who call. Among the tasks of the pak-ke is to select a group of young unmarried men and women between the ages of seventeen and twenty-five to teach younger children about courting. In particular this includes learning polite speeches and rhymes. The pak-ke also oversee a ceremony called the "*prüh,*" the taming or teaching of children (Milne 1924: 62–70). The prüh includes a lottery in which boys and girls are matched and the boy is subsequently expected to pay visits to the girl for the next few months. An important sign of transition for young girls is the donning of a skirt rather than trousers and for a boy it is being tattooed. Milne (1924: 96) comments that boys who put off being tattooed are taunted by boys who have already been tattooed and by girls: "'Thou are a girl', or 'Thou are a pumpkin, smooth all over', or 'Thou art a Chinaman'—the Chinese do not tattoo."

Courting in earnest begins around the time a girl is fourteen and a boy is fifteen or sixteen and Milne (1924: 128) notes that girls rarely marry before they are sixteen to eighteen and sometimes not until they are twenty-five or older. They are reported generally to marry older men. Parents are expected for the most part not to interfere in young people's courting and a couple can decide to marry without their parents knowing or giving their consent. The marriage itself takes different forms. In Tawngpeng and some other areas it involves elopement, but other groups (including the Silver Palaung of southern Shan State) only practice elopement when the parents disapprove of the marriage and generally consider such behavior highly inappropriate. Marriage negotiations take place to establish a payment from the groom's family which goes toward helping to pay for the wedding feast. The bride takes a dowry with her comprised of clothing and various household items.

Funeral arrangements depend on the cause of death and the status of the deceased. In the case of what are considered abnormal deaths (e.g., by violence, from being struck by lightning, or as a result of childbirth), the deceased is quickly buried in an isolated location without a coffin. If the deceased is a monk or elderly noble the body is cremated with the form of cremation following Burmese Buddhist practices. Cameron (1912: 22–5) reports that other notables such as clan chiefs and village headmen also are sometimes cremated. Commoners who die a normal death are buried in a coffin in an unmarked grave in the village cemetery. Silver Palaung villages have cemeteries which they call *parlor*. The body is washed and dressed before being placed in the coffin. Usually burial takes place on the same day as the death or, in the case of death at night, the next morning or soon thereafter. On the day of the burial and for the next week, a group of elderly men gather in the house of the deceased to chant Buddhist scriptures. Offerings of food are also taken to the temple to be placed before the Buddha image and given to monks. On the seventh day, after a final offering of food, the spirit of the deceased is called upon to depart.

SOCIAL AND POLITICAL ORGANIZATION

The primary social group among the Palaung is the nuclear family, often along with one or more other relatives such as a widowed parent or unmarried sibling. After marriage and before a couple's new house is built or they are able to move into their own room in a multiple-family house, they usually live with the groom's parents for a time. Long houses commonly have up to six and in some accounts up to twenty families living in them. Each family unit has its own living quarters with its own fireplace and section of the porch or hallway. The existing literature does not discuss relationships among the families living in such long houses. In Tawngping, where Milne worked there were no long houses. Data collected from the Silver Palaung who do have them indicates that those living together in a long house do not have to be related, the main criteria being simply that they get along with one another. Those living in a long house are expected to cooperate when necessary and to listen to and respect the wishes of the senior residents.

The primary kin-based group among the Palaung beyond the level of the family is commonly referred to in the literature as the clan. Early writers on the Palaung such as Milne use the term clan, but their descriptions of the nature of these clans is rather ambiguous. The term refers to something more akin to a sub-tribe or ethnolinguistic sub-group than what is commonly thought of as a clan in the anthropological literature. These are named groups that in some instances occupy a residentially distinct area, but often are widely scattered. In regard to the latter, the members of such groups may at one time have occupied a discrete area, but over time for various reasons migrated and become dispersed. The Palaung view their clans as having distinct dialects and cultural traditions in regard to such things as marriage practices and women's dress. There appear to be about fifteen Palaung clans or ethnolinguistic sub-groups in Burma.

Scott and Hardiman (1900: 486) mention that one clan, the Pato Ru, or the "tribe of the centre," lays claim to being "the Rumai proper." They inhabit the village of Tawng Ma, south of Namhsan, and this village is said to be the oldest in the state. This clan apparently at one time was comprised entirely of relatives of the rulers of Tawngpeng and practiced clan endogamy. Among the exclusive privileges claimed by members of this clan in the past was the right of their male members alone among Rumai men to wear colored clothing. Men of other Rumai clans were allowed to wear only plain black and white clothing. Scott and Hardiman note, however, that at the time of their writing "these differences have vanished. There are no such restrictions, and members of all clans intermarry so freely that seemingly the old distinctions have vanished."

For centuries the Palaung were integrated into the feudal principalities of the Shan, called *müang,* or what Leach (1954) refers to as a *gumsa* political system. These were ruled over by a prince known as a chaofa or sawbwa. Below the chaofa was a *kem-müang,* the designated heir to the throne. Müang were divided into districts, called *myoza,* a Burmese term adopted by the Shan. The rulers of myoza, commonly brothers and sons of the chaofa, were called *chao khun müang.* There were further sub-divisions comprised of large groups of villages, then smaller groups of villages, and, finally, single villages. The heads of these were called *paw müang* (or *tao müang* or *pu haeng*), *pu müang,* and *pu kae* (or *pu kang*), respectively. The courts of the chaofa also had a number of officials with administrative and ceremonial roles.

Milne (1924: 18) refers to two Palaung chronicles, the "Namhsan Chronicle" of the ruler of Tawngpeng and another of the "Kangwantok Palê," which trace the origin of the Palaung to the hills around the Shan town of "Se-lan," near Namh Kam. Se-lan is said to have fallen to the Chinese, resulting in the Palaung moving further south. Milne speculates "that Se-lan may have been the capital of a State where the Shans lived in the valleys and the Palaungs in the hills," but warns that the legends in the chronicles may simply have been borrowed from the Shan.

After the legendary fall of Se-lan the Palaung are said to have wandered through Wa territory. Milne comments that the accounts of these migrations resemble "the narrative of the life and wanderings of the Israelites" (Milne 1924: 19). In the Namhsan Chronicle the Palaung eventually settle in the Tawgpeng area after the leader of the Palaung discovers water there by thrusting a bamboo pole in the ground.

Tawngpeng eventually became established as a state in the Shan fashion, but it was ruled over by a Palaung. Elsewhere, the Palaung lived within Shan states ruled over by Shan. The Silver Palaung are to be found living primarily in three of the southern müang (or states), from west to east: Yawng Hwe (Yawnghwe), Mong Nai (Muang Nai), and Keng Tung (Kengtung). From the mid-eighteenth century until the coming of the British in the 1880s Tawngpeng and the other Shan states were under Burmese rule. This meant that the local rulers paid tribute annually to the Burmese king in Ava and later Mandalay.

Milne provides accounts of fights among various individuals seeking to rule over Tawngpeng during the nineteenth century prior to British rule (Milne 1924: 20–2). In these struggles there are instances of the contenders employing Jingpho troops and turning to the Burmese king for help against a rival. Between 1836 and the early 1840s such struggles seem to have created chaos throughout Tawngpeng. To add to the troubles, in 1841 Burmese troops entered the state and laid waste to many of the villages and monasteries. A man named "K'un S'a" established himself as ruler, but his reign seems to have been a tyrannical one. He killed those he perceived to be his rivals and "was a terror to the women of the country; for, although he had thirty wives, when he saw a pretty girl and wished to add her to his household, he threatened that if she did not conform willingly to his wishes, her father and mother should be put to death" (Milne 1924: 21). K'un S'a was finally killed in 1860 and his palace and surrounding buildings were destroyed. Milne notes that while K'un S'a "seems to have the worst reputation" of all the rulers of Tawngpeng, "yet I have met many Palaungs who admire him for his fearlessness" (22).

After a few years of fighting over who would replace K'un S'a, a man named "K'un Kam Kon" (k'un or khun is used as a title) assumed the throne with the blessing of the Burmese king. He died after one year, however, and was succeeded by his elder brother, "K'un Kam Möng," in 1877. Kam Mong ruled until 1887, when he abdicated in favor of his son, "K'un Kyang. It was at this time that British rule was established over the Shan states, including Tawngpeng. As noted by Scott and Hardiman (1900: 302) in regard to British rule over the Shan states, "the intention of the Government [was] to maintain order and to prevent private wars between the several States, while at the same time allowing to each Chief independence in the administration of his territory to the fullest extent compatible with the methods of civilized government." In short, the British established a structure of indirect rule. Each ruler was recognized separately and placed under the suzerainty of the governor of India. Now under indirect British control,

2.7. "Girls carrying offerings to the image-house."
From Milne (1924), facing p. 326.

K'un Kyang continued to rule over Tawngpeng until he died in 1897. Since his children were very young, the throne was offered to his brother, K'un Lu. K'un Lu turned down the offer and suggested that the title be given to his cousin, K'un S'ang. This was done and K'un S'ang accepted. He was then recognized by the British and was still the ruler when Milne conducted her study (and, one may assume, was the man who initially invited her to come to Tawngpeng).

The chaofa retained almost complete power over local affairs until colonial reforms in 1922, which created the Federated Shan States. A commissioner was appointed over this new entity with power over a central budget. There were also the usual departments that were part of a colonial administrative structure. The chaofa's powers under this new arrangement were greatly reduced. As Chao Tzang Yawnghwe (1987: 79) remarks, "their status was severely reduced . . . to that of poorly paid but elevated native tax-collectors."

For most Palaung living in their villages, the chaofa was a distant and not overly relevant figure. As one descendant of the ruling family of the müang of Yawnghwe notes: "even under the 'feudal' scheme of things, Shan peasants were, in the European sense, freemen, and in village and local matters, governed themselves" (Yawnghwe 1987: 82). Of more direct relevance to Palaung villagers were the sub-district officers such as the paw müang, pu müang, and pu kae. In predominantly Palaung areas these positions appear to have been filled by Palaung. Cameron (1912: 33–4) describes the Palaung and Rumai in Muang Mit. He mentions clan chiefs who oversaw groups of villages, a position like that of the paw müang, and under them heads of smaller groups of villages and village headmen. Cameron states that on the death of the incumbent, the position of clan chief usually went to the oldest living member of the clan, but that the choice was up to the elders of the clan, who notified the chaofa in Muang Mit. The position of village headman was decided upon by the members of a village and confirmed by the clan chief. While major infractions of the law were handled by the clan chiefs, minor matters were dealt with by the village headmen. The headmen were also responsible for collecting tribute due to the chaofa from fellow villagers.

RELIGIOUS BELIEFS AND PRACTICES

The Palaung are Buddhists who also worship a variety of spirits (*nats* in Burmese terminology). According to oral history in Tawngpeng, Theravada Buddhism was introduced to the Palaung in 1782, when the Burmese king sent a monk to Tawngpeng. Milne (1924: 312) believes, however, that the Palaung knew of Buddhism prior to this since it had been introduced to the Shan in adjacent states over two centuries earlier. In fact, the Palaung have a history of being influenced by both Shan and Burmese Buddhists. This is reflected in the existence of two schools of Buddhism among the Palaung: the Burmese school among northern Palaung and the Yun (Shan) school among other Palaung, including the Silver Palaung. The primary difference between these schools is that the Yun school features a series of grades for monks which is absent in the Burmese school. The passage upward into each new grade is marked by increasingly elaborate ceremonies, the costs of which are borne by the monk's relatives and godparents.

Milne (1924: 336–42, 355–60) provides the most detailed account available of Palaung beliefs concerning spirits. The Golden Palaung studied by Milne believe in a variety of spirits, known generally as *kar-nam,* who live in such natural features as large trees, hills, and rocks. There are also guardian spirits of the house, village, roads and paths, and important crops such as tea and rice. Individuals are believed to have two personal spirits, known as *kar-bu* and *vin-yin.* The kar-bu is a spirit possessed by all animals, while the vin-yin is viewed as the intelligent and immortal part of humans. The latter is probably of Buddhist origin. Upon death, the spirits of humans and animals generally linger for about a week, seeking a new host for reincarnation. Not all kar-bu follow this path. Thus, kar-bu of humans suffering violent death become kar-nam. Such kar-nam of human origin are considered to be particularly malevolent. Other kar-bu become *pe-aet,* a type of ghost with vaguely human form that can materialize at will and pass through solid objects. There are also an assortment of other supernatural beings, such as *pok* (who live upon the dead) and ogres, who Milne believes are of Burmese origin.

In addition to Buddhist monks there are religious specialists among the Palaung linked to these non-Buddhist supernatural beings. These specialists include the *hsa-ra,* a diviner and medical practitioner and often tattooer. The advice of a hsa-ra is sought when naming a child, selecting a house site, and orienting the house. A person may also pay a hsa-ra for amulets or incantations to help in love or seeking revenge. There are also *bre,* witches, whose spirit can possess the body of another. This ability is passed from mother to daughter and witches usually live in separate parts of a village. The court at Tawngpeng also had a hereditary priest, known as the *ta pleng* (grandfather or old man of the sky), who served as an intermediary in dealing with spirits. Silver Palaung villages usually have a spirit priest known as a *tha eel muon.*

In discussing spirits with Palaung in Thailand, they knew about kar-nam as spirits of trees, plants, and the like. They also used the terms vin-yin and *karpraw* for human and animal spirits, but tended to treat these as essentially the same thing. Those who die a violent death are said to become kar-nam. Bre are viewed as men and women who have been possessed by evil spirits. Such people are said to have distinctive physical attributes: e.g., their hair stands up and their eyes are very red. Expelling the spirit that has possessed such a person is done by puncturing the body with a sharp object such as a tiger tooth.

The Palaung celebrate the major ceremonies associated with Buddhism. There was also a tradition of celebrating an annual state spirit festival in Tawngpeng in September, at which the ta pleng and his assistants summon all of the Palaung spirits to receive offerings after a large public gathering attended by members of the populace at large as well as royals, elders, and monks.

In addition to various forest monasteries and those in urban centers, virtually every Palaung village has a monastery compound. There are also a variety of structures erected for the spirits. Milne (1924: 345) notes that there are many "kar-nam shrines" in the forest. She describes them as follows: "A small house, almost like a doll's house, two or three feet in height and the same width, is set on poles under some great tree at a distance from a path. It is roughly put together of split bamboos, and a small fence of a few upright and horizontal poles encloses both tree and shrine." She goes on to comment that while "a Burman or a Shan will step boldly into the enclosure of a spirit-shrine . . . no Palaung will enter its precincts without bringing an offering." As was noted earlier when discussing settlement patterns, she also says, without going into detail, that villages sometimes have "a more substantial shrine" for the "spirit-guardian" of the village. Among the Silver Palaung such a shrine for the village's spirit-guardian is called a *demoo müang*.

1. Hills near Kalaw being planted with tea by Silver Palaung (Jan. 1999)

2. Silver Palaung village near Kalaw (Jan. 1999)

3. Silver Palaung village main street, near Kalaw (Jan. 1999)

4. Silver Palaung village heart,
near Kalaw (Jan. 1999)

Pl. 5. Silver Palaung woman making
a basket, near Kalaw (Jan. 1999)

6. The last Silver Palaung long house in the Kalaw area (Jan. 1999)

7. Silver Palaung village shrine near Kalaw (Jan. 99)

8. Old Silver Palaung couple (the man is village priest), near Kalaw (Jan. 1999)

9. Thai border post at No Lae, facing Burma (Dec. 1998)

10. House in No Lae (Dec. 1998)

11. No Lae village (Dec. 1998)

12. Village heart, No Lae
(Dec. 1998)

13. Verandah scene, No Lae (Dec. 1998)

14. Young girl, No Lae
(Dec. 1998)

15. Married women with children, No Lae (Dec. 1998)

16. Older women wearing black headcloths, No Lae (Dec. 1998)

17. House, Pang Daeng Nai (Jan. 1998)

18. Village shrine, Pang Daeng Nai (July 1998)

19. Verandah scene, Pang Daeng Nai (Dec. 1998)

20. Village heart, Pang Daeng Nai (Jan. 1998)

21. Young boy, Pang Daeng Nai (Jan. 1998)

22. Young girls, Pang Daeng Nai (Dec. 1998)

23. Preparing yarn to weave,
Pang Daeng Nai (Jan. 1998)

24. Weaving, Pang Daeng Nai (Jan. 1998)

25. Weaving, Pang Daeng Nai (Jan. 1998)

26. Kam-hieng, Pang Daeng Nai (Feb. 1998)

27. Young woman, Pang Daeng Nai (Feb. 1998)

28. Kam-hieng cooking beans, Pang Daeng Nai (Feb. 1998)

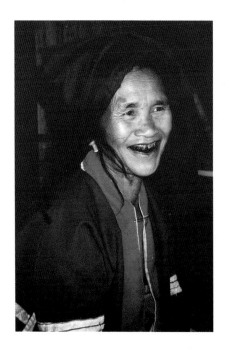

29. Older woman with black
headcloth, Pang Daeng Nai
(Jan. 1998)

30. Village headman, Huai Pong
(Feb. 1998)

31. Young men, Pang Daeng Nok (Feb. 1998)

CHAPTER 3

DRESS AND IDENTITY

We now turn to a discussion of Palaung dress. It was after all this topic which originally brought us to the Palaung and it is the most noticeable physical indicator of Palaung ethnic identity both in Burma and in Thailand. Palaung female dress is easily differentiated from that of neighboring peoples and is frequently cited by Palaung as well as non-Palaung as an important marker of Palaung ethnic identity. Especially distinct is the hood traditionally worn by Palaung women in Namhsan and the headcloth traditionally worn by Silver Palaung women. The skirts too, although relatively plain, are different from those worn by neighboring Shan, Karen, and others. Palaung women have continued to wear their distinctive dress in Thailand and to weave the cloth for their skirts. Thus, female dress remains a significant ethnic identifier for Palaung living in Thailand that sets them apart from the Thai majority and from other minority groups in the north of the country.

THE DRESS OF NEIGHBORING MON-KHMER
SPEAKING PEOPLES

As was discussed in the previous chapter, the Palaung who are the focus of the present study speak Northern Mon-Khmer languages. Before proceeding with a discussion of the dress of the various Palaung groups we feel that it is useful to look at the dress of other neighboring Northern Mon-Khmer speaking peoples for comparative purposes. In general, the peoples speaking these languages have relatively simple traditions of textile production and their patterns of dress and weaving techniques are often influenced by neighboring, especially Tai-speaking, groups. More detailed information on the dress of these Mon-Khmer speaking groups is available in Howard (1999).

The languages of these peoples can be divided into Palaungic and Khmuic languages. The Palaung groups discussed in the remainder of the chapter speak Eastern Palaungic languages. The other group speaking an Eastern Palaungic language are the Riang. Closely related linguistically to the Palaung and Riang are the Western Palaungic languages of the Wa, Blang, Samtao, Tai Loi, and Lawa. The Khmuic languages include only the Khmu in Burma.

3.1. A group of Riang women belonging to the Yang-Sek clan.
From Scott (1921), facing p. 140.

The Riang live in the southern part of Shan State and include the Riang themselves (who are known also as Black Karen) as well as the closely related Yinchia (who are also called Striped Karen or Black Riang). There are three Riang clans identified by Shan names: Yang Lam, Yang Sek, and Yang Wan-hkun. The Yang Lam were closest to the Shan and Scott (1921: 139) observed that all Yang Lam men wore Shan dress, as did an increasing number of the women. The traditional female dress of the Yang Lam is described by Scott as consisting of an ankle-length dark indigo tubeskirt made of homespun cotton and a jacket with no front or side openings, of the same color and material (139). The only additional color is "an insertion of scarlet at the bosom." He also notes that they sometimes wear no headdress.

Riang women of the Yang Sek and Yang Wan-hkun clans are described by Scott (1921: 140) as having distinctive and more colorful dress than Yang Lam women. Yang Wan-hkun women's dress is described as follows:

> The skirt is of the same dark blue homespun, but it is elaborately flounced—the only instance of this feature of dressmaking among the milliners of Burma, and probably in the East generally. The dress is much shorter, probably to show the black-lacquer garters below the knee. The basis of the jacket is also indigo-blue cloth, but it is elaborately embroidered, and ornamented with beads and scarlet *appliqué*. Coils of thin bamboo or cane rings, varnished with wood oil, are worn round the waist.

Scott (1921: 140) states that Yang Sek women wear a Karen-like poncho "with perpendicular red and white stripes" and "garter rings of brass wire." Woodthorpe (1897: 27) describes these ponchos as "curious long coats like sacks with holes for head and arms with very short sleeves with alternate white and red longitudinal stripes."

There are a few Riang textiles in the collection of Göteborg's Ethnographical Museum: two from the Yang Sek clan and four from the Yang Lam clan. These are described in Hansen (1960). The Yang Sek textiles include a woman's sleeveless gown that is decorated in the center with tassels made of lace and cords in green and purple, and a man's jacket with sleeves made of plain white cotton. The Yang Lam textiles include a woman's tubeskirt made of black cotton; a woman's sleeveless blouse made of plain black cotton cloth with a border of bright red cloth added at the bottom and decorations of tassels, ribbons, and fringe added on the sides, center, and across the bottom; a woman's headcloth made of orange-colored cotton with red horizontal stripes; and a man's trousers made of indigo-dyed cotton cloth.

Scott and Hardiman (1900: 510) and Scott (1921: 136–7) are the primary published sources on Wa dress in Burma. These and other sources published during the early twentieth century distinguish between the dress of the more northerly Wa (sometimes called the Wild Wa) and the more southerly ones (sometimes called the Tame Wa). The former were autonomous and little influenced by external cultures, while the latter were strongly influenced by Shan culture and lived within the Shan political system.

Scott (1921: 135) describes Tame Wa men as wearing either Shan dress or loincloths and, sometimes, a blanket. He notes that there are distinctive patterns in the loincloths associated with particular subgroups. Such loincloths are described as being "striped or chequered in various patterns, or in different colours, for the so-called clans." Scott describes Tame Wa women merely as wearing "skirts and jackets" (137). The impression is that the cloth for these items of clothing is relatively plain with only a little simple decorative patterning.

From the various descriptions available, Wild Wa dress is even simpler. During warm weather, Scott and Hardiman (1900: 510) and Scott (1921: 136–7) comment that both men and women go about naked, wearing only a few ornaments. On ceremonial occasions Wild Wa men are described as wearing a narrow and relatively plain loincloth: "a strip of coarse cotton about three fingers broad" (Scott and Hardiman 1900: 510) with tassels at the end. Cold weather wear includes a blanket that is worn over the shoulders, described by Scott and Hardiman as "a coarse home-woven coverlet." Wild Wa women wear a skirt in cold weather when outside the village grounds which, according to Scott (1921: 136), "is none too long if worn extended, but is usually worn doubled up, and is then all too short." Skirts, blankets, and loincloths of the Wild Wa seem to have been relatively plain, even more so than those of the Tame Wa, and examples of Wa clothing in museum collections have only a few plain stripes by way of decoration.

There are no published descriptions of the dress of the Blang in Burma, but there are descriptions of Blang dress in neighboring areas of China (where there are many more Blang). *Ethnic Costumes and Clothing Decorations from China* (Shanghai Theatrical College 1986: 198) describes Blang men as wearing clothing common to men in other groups: black long-sleeved, collarless jackets that open from the front, black loose trousers, and black or white cotton headcloths. Blang women's dress is more distinctive (198–9). They wear close-fitting, collarless jackets with long sleeves that are fastened on one side and have a bell-bottom lower hem with a patterned strip. Younger girls wear light pink or green jackets, while older women wear black ones. Women may also wear a close-fitting blouse under the jacket. The women wear two tubeskirts. The inner skirt is usually a light color and the outer features horizontal stripes in red, black, white, and occasionally other colors. The inner skirt alone is worn when at home or working in the fields. The outer skirt is added for special occasions. Leggings are also worn sometimes. Adult women wear large turbans made of black or blue-green cloth that are decorated with tassels at the ends. Both men and women also carry shoulder bags that are predominately white with some ornamentation. Their dress is therefore relatively simple, patterning on the skirts being limited essentially to plain horizontal lines, and the style of female blouse is influenced by Chinese fashion.

There are only a small number of Samtao in Burma and no published descriptions of their dress. There are also Samtao in Laos, and Chazee (1995: 91) reports that the Samtao there are strongly influenced by the Lue and that the designs employed on their woven cloth resemble those of the Lue.

Some authors consider the Tai Loi to be Wa who have adopted many aspects of Tai culture (Scott and Hardiman 1900: 517; Davies 1909: 373–4) and they are often referred to as "hill Shans." Davies (1909: 374–5) describes Tai Loi men as dressing "in the universal dark blue of the Chinaman" and the women wearing "dark blue jackets ornamented with a little red, and with shell ornaments hanging down the front" and skirts that are "usually striped with red, blue, or yellow." Chazee

(1995: 51) states that the traditional dress of the Tai Loi in Laos disappeared generations ago and that they have adopted the dress of the Tai speaking Lue and Lao.

There is surprisingly little literature on the dress of the Lawa (or Lua') of northern Thailand. Like the Palaung, but even more surprisingly, the Lawa are generally ignored in surveys of hill tribe material culture, although they do feature in more general works on the hill tribes of northern Thailand. An exhibition catalogue by Kunstadter, Harmon, and Kunstadter (1978) provides some information on their textiles, and Sylvia Fraser-Lu (1988: 122) gives a brief description of their dress. She describes Lawa men as dressing "in a manner similar to lowland Thai farmers in indigo-coloured shirts and loose-fitting pants." Women are described as wearing a "a white or blue sleeveless blouse, which is loose, bulky, and similar in cut to that of the Karen tribe," a short tubeskirt "patterned with naturally dyed blue and red warp stripes of varying thickness, some of which enclose small dot and dash patterns of warp ikat in 'lightning' motifs," and leggings. Although she does not say so, the tubeskirts also are similar to those produced by neighboring Karen. They also make blankets, used mainly for ceremonial purposes, that include some warp ikat and supplementary weft patterning (see color photograph in Howard 1994, p. 190, no. 88). Thus, Lawa weaving is somewhat more sophisticated that of other nearby Mon-Khmer groups. This appears to be the result of the influence of the Karen who live in the same general vicinity.

Scott and Hardiman (1900: 521) mention three Khmuic speaking sub-groups living in Burma near the border with Laos: the Hka Muk, Hka Met, and Hka Kwen. They remark that these sub-groups "have different fashions of dress, but the variations do not seem to be very great." The men of these sub-groups are described as dressing like the Shan: "in blue or white coats, buttoning on the right side, and blue trousers" and occasionally headcloths or "Shan hats with no turban." They describe Khmu women as wearing "petticoats with horizontal stripes of colours differing with the tribes, and near the Mèkhong all have sleeveless coats of blue cloth which fail to reach the top of the petticoat." Unfortunately, they do not provide information as to specifically what these different colors are or with which sub-group they are associated. Such an association of different patterns of stripes with sub-group identity, as we will see below, is also common to the Palaung.

The Wa are the only group above for which men are noted to have worn loincloths. It is likely, however, that men of all of these groups (including the Palaung) in the distant past wore such loincloths, but centuries of Tai, Chinese, and Burman influence has resulted in male dress taking on relatively uniform characteristics that reflect such external influences. Female dress has remained somewhat more distinctive despite its relative simplicity, but even here it is common for female dress among these Mon-Khmer speaking groups to closely resemble that of their neighbors.

THE LITERATURE ON PALAUNG DRESS

References to Palaung dress begin with Yule (1858) who cites a couple of rather unhelpful reports about the Palaung being "good dyers" (149) and, presumably the men, wearing "breeches" (275). The latter comment was perhaps intended to distinguish them from groups where the men wore loincloths.

Scott and Hardiman (1900) provide a good deal more information. After noting "that the men at any rate have all adopted the Shan dress" (487), they proceed to describe the distinctive dress of the women. They describe Palaung female dress, probably in the Namhsan area, as follows:

> The ordinary every-day dress of the women is a dark-blue cut-away jacket and a skirt and blue leggings. The full dress is much brighter in colour. A large hood is worn, which is brought to a point at the back of the head and reaches down over the shoulders. The border is white with an inner patch-work pattern of blue, scarlet, and black cotton velvet. The skirt is often composed of panels of cotton velvet of these various colours with garters to match, and the general effect is very gay . . . Round the wrist [I suspect they mean waist] are worn numbers of black varnished bamboo hoops of the same character as those of the Kachins, sometimes

plain, sometimes decked with cowries and seeds. Some women do not wear these, but whether because they are inconvenient or because it denotes a clan distinction has not been ascertained.

There is also a photograph of a woman said to be "Rumai or Palaung" (1900: facing p. 569, pl. xv). They describe the dress of Pale women (1900: 487) as comprised of "a hood which is entirely white, with a short dark-blue coat and a skirt striped horizontally with red and blue."

3.2. "Rumai or Palaung woman." From Scott and Hardiman (1900), pl. XV, facing p. 569.

Scott and Hardiman (1900: 486) discuss dress distinctions among the Pato Ru clan. The authors describe this clan as being Rumai, but it is more likely that they are the initial Golden Palaung residents of Tawngpeng and are the clan of the founding ruling dynasty of that state. Among the exclusive privileges claimed by members of this clan at one time was the right of their male members alone among Palaung men to wear colored clothing. Men of other clans were allowed to wear only plain black and white clothing. Scott and Hardiman note, however, that at the time of their writing "these differences have vanished. There are no such restrictions, and members of all clans intermarry so freely that seemingly the old distinctions have vanished." It may be the vanishing of these specific clan distinctions that the authors are referring to elsewhere in their entry on the Palaung when they claim (erroneously) that clan distinctions in dress generally have vanished.

Scott and Hardiman (1900: 489) describe the use of certain items of cloth in the wooing activities of young Palaung. This includes a young man sending to a young woman whose name he has drawn by lot gifts that include a silk handkerchief. The young woman reciprocates with gifts consisting of "a tasseled cloth, a sort of connecting link between a towel and a handkerchief, and a belt worked by herself." The receipt of these gifts indicates that the young man may go ahead and "press his suit in person." Milne (1924) provides a more detailed account of such wooing activities.

Earlier in their gazetteer Scott and Hardiman (1900: 366) also discuss the impact of imported cloth and the decline of weaving among the Palaung of Tawngpeng:

> The Palaungs of Tawng Peng Loi Lông buy their threads already dyed from the hawkers, or traders, or in a bazaar. Imported fabrics have certainly reduced the amount of weaving done, and as the country becomes civilized the weaving will still further decrease. The locally-made cloth being infinitely more durable, it is cheaper to wear clothes made from it, but the richer Palaungs of Nam San and the surrounding villages that are nearer civilization prefer something finer in appearance. It is only amongst the poorer classes that weaving is now done.

3.3. "Daughter and little son of the chief of Tawngpeng." Drawing based on a photograph in Milne (1924), facing p. 212.

Subsequent studies prior to Milne's major ethnography are short on detail about Palaung dress and add little to what Scott and Hardiman have to say. Davies (1909: 376), for example, remarks that the turban worn by Palaung women "is different from that of the Kachin women, and does not stick up so high." Milne herself in her 1910 monograph on the Shan provides a brief description of Palaung female dress (1910: 135). She describes their jacket as being loose-fitting and generally made of "home-woven stuff" that is usually "dull of colour" except at festivals when it is "made of bright blue velvet faced with scarlet." She notes that the skirts are worn with cane hoops around the waist and sometimes a silver belt and that women may also wear indigo gaiters. The description of Palaung dress given by Scott in his handbook on Burma (1921: 132) is much the same as that appearing in his earlier gazetteer entry. Also, he continues to treat the Rumai and Palaung as the same group and his descriptions refer primarily to the Golden Palaung of Tawngpeng. His account is accompanied by a photo (facing p. 132) with the caption reading simply "Palaungs" (see fig. 1.2). From the women's skirts and headdresses it would appear that the photo is of either Rumai or Silver Palaung and most likely the latter.

We are provided our first really detailed description of Palaung dress in Leslie Milne's 1924 monograph. She describes the skirts (*klang*) as having horizontal stripes, which vary in color and width according to clan, but provides no specifics. She then describes, in remarkable detail in comparison with her contemporaries, the remainder of what appears to be the attire of an affluent female (209, 212, 213):

Over this garment [the skirt] is the *re-twai,* in two parts, tied round the waist with strings that are hidden by silver chains. The front part is not unlike an apron. The back part is much wider; it covers the back of the skirt and overlaps the front part of the waist. Both are made of several horizontal strips, which for young women, girls, and girl-children may be of any brightly coloured stuff or of silk. The lower border of both parts is composed of a patchwork of rectangular pieces of a heavier material in two colours, usually orange and purple or orange and green, arranged alternately. At each of the lower corners hang two or more tufts of brightly coloured wool. The smock (*ka-pro*), which only reaches to the waist, may be of velvet or silk of any colour; it has short scarlet sleeves, and usually there is a scarlet horizontal panel in front and a narrow border of scarlet round the V-shaped opening for the neck. The under-sleeves (*kar-ti*)—generally of silk or velvet—which cover the forearm are not attached to the smock and are removed when work is to be done. The head is always covered with a loosely fitting black velvet cap (*hmok*), usually adorned with silver ornaments of coiled wire (*hma-e*). Above and partly hiding this is worn the hood (*ra-ngu-i*). This hood, for an adult, is about fifty-two inches in length and a yard in width. It consists of a rectangular piece of material folded and joined at the top to form a covering for the head; the rest of the garment hangs loosely over the shoulders and back. A narrow border of plush or velvet frames the face. Down either side and along the bottom there is a wide border, generally of flowered silk, which may be of any colour. There is a large panel at the back of the head, and a narrow horizontal panel on the back below the waist. These may be of any coloured material, or they may be ornamented with gold or silver embroidery in which are set imitation gems in a multitude of spangles. The greater part of the hood is of scarlet cloth, made up of different-sized panels. The garment is supposed to represent a Naga's skin, the panels being the scales . . . A curious little patch of black velvet is generally sewn on the top. There is a good deal of embroidery on all the garments, with stitches so fine as to be almost invisible on the silk or in the pile of the velvet . . . The long hood is lined throughout with unbleached cotton cloth. The leggings (*kar-jüng*) are squares of indigo-blue cotton or brightly coloured velvet. They are folded round the leg and are fastened with strings twisted round from ankle to knee.

Her description is accompanied by seven drawings of embroidery designs (1924: 210–3) and a photo of the "daughter and little son of the chief of Tawngpeng" (facing p. 212) that is the inspiration for the drawing in the present text (fig. 3.4). Her account of Palaung dress also includes a discussion about women's hair (213):

> False hair is never worn by the Palaungs; but the women often cut off
> their hair and sell it to the Shans, who do not disdain to add to their

tresses. Palaung women often cut their hair quite short; but when their hair is long, they wear it hanging straight down the back, not tied or fastened in any way. It is not seen when they are out of doors, as it is covered by the hood. Occasionally, at festivals, girls wear a lock of hair hanging down on each side in front, over the shoulders.

Milne focuses on the Golden Palaung of Tawngpeng. However, there are photos in her monograph of a Rumai woman (facing p. 370) and a "Palê girl spinning" (facing p. 138), but no accompanying description of their dress.

Scattered throughout her work are references to social and ceremonial aspects of dress. Milne (1924: 62–4) describes the ceremony whereby a young girl around the age of nine or ten ceases to wear trousers like a boy and dons a skirt for the first time. She also discusses clothing in relation to marriage. Thus, "when a girl becomes engaged to be married, she asks her lover to give her enough money to buy a couple of dresses . . . The engaged girl on receiving the money promises in return to be faithful to her vows of betrothal" (117). Actually what they purchase is material to make dresses. The dresses themselves are made by friends of the girl out of the sight of her mother "so that the girl's mother may not wonder why her daughter is making so many new clothes." Buying the cloth for the trousseau is described as follows:

> When she begins to buy the things, she pretends to her mother that she is going to help another girl choose cloth; she tries, if possible, to begin making any purchases at the time of the full moon, as that day brings good luck. There is much to buy: cloth and silk; satin and velvet; thread of various colours, white, black, red, green, and yellow; sometimes—but more rarely—thread that is blue and lilac in colour; worsted of various colours; also skeins of silk. Girls take a long time to make their purchases, and look over the stock of all the traders in the place; Burmans, Shans, and natives of India have the principal shops for cloth.

After the girl has eloped with her lover and her parents have agreed to the marriage, her mother calls on two of the girl's friends and asks them to take her daughter the new clothes that have been made: "She left her home in an old dress and a shabby hood, but I have found among her things some new clothes; please take them to her" (1924: 151). Later, the girl is also given a new set of clothing by her mother-in-law (153).

3.4. "Palê girl spinning." From Milne (1924), facing p. 138.

There is a discussion (Milne 1924: 229) about clothing worn while picking tea. This is described as hard and messy work since it often takes place when it is raining heavily. Both men and women are described as wearing "capes made from the leaves of the screw-pine-tree." However, while the men are able to roll up their trousers and take off their shirts if it is warm enough, the women can do little as their clothing becomes soaked in the rain: "If a girl tries to protect her clothing from the rain, by turning up her garments to the knee, she is chaffed by her companions, who call her a Kachin." In an accompanying footnote the author comments that Kachin wear skirts that are very short and "are looked down upon by Palaungs because they are not Buddhists."

In regard to burial customs, Milne (1924: 292) notes that the body of the deceased is fully clothed. The body is put in a coffin with the head placed on a pillow that is covered with colored velvet or plain white cotton. The body is then covered with a piece of cloth: "If the family is rich, a velvet cloth may cover the body; if poor, a strip of white homespun cotton cloth is used." Milne also states that when the deceased is unmarried, a rope is stretched over the coffin from one end of the room to the other. To it "men attach their turbans, hats, swords, and new handkerchiefs to one part, while girls hang their hoods on the rope on another part" (293). The belief is that by doing this they will ensure that the dead person has many friends in the next life. When the coffin is taken to the burial ground these items are placed on the coffin lid or on a platform or poles attached to the bier (297). The items are removed before the mourners reach the burial ground and may be worn afterwards.

For the most part, accounts of the Palaung dress appearing in works published after Milne's monograph add nothing significant. Stevenson (1944: 14), for example, provides only a very brief general description: women are described as wearing jackets which are blue with red collars and relatively short skirts. Based on early twentieth century sources, Lebar, Hickey, and Musgrave (1964: 123) report that men's clothing was already made of imported cloth. In regard to women's clothing, they note that some women still wove their own cloth, but that even the handmade cloth usually came from the Shan, although Palaung women did embroider on the cloth.

Useful comparative data is provided in the Shanghai Theatrical College's (1986) survey of ethnic dress in China. There are a number of color photos and drawings in the section on the Chinese De'ang (see pp. 216–21). De'ang men are described as wearing indigo or brown jackets that open from the side, short indigo trousers, and a white turban with colorful woolen balls at the ends—somewhat different from the dress of neighboring Tai men. Women of the different groups within the De'ang, as noted earlier in the chapter, are reported to wear distinctive skirts: "Women of the Red De'ang branch wear skirts with red horizontal stripes. Floral De'ang women's skirts are evenly woven with red and black or red and blue horizontal stripes; the Black De'angs' skirts are woven of black threads with fine stripes of red and white in between them. The majority of photos appear to illustrate Floral De'ang women, although this is not stated. One photo (p. 221, no. 532) provides an illustration of the dress of the Red De'ang and states the affiliation in the caption. In this case the upper two-thirds of the skirt is plain black and the lower portion features a wide horizontal red band and below it a plain black band, with thin red and white stripes at the top and bottom of this lower portion.

The authors also make note of the different style of jackets of particular groups: "the Red and Floral De'ang women wear blue or black jackets open in the front with silver buttons; the front border is trimmed with two strips of red cloth and the border of the bottom is decorated with small red, green, and yellow balls. Married women of Black De'ang . . . wear jackets open from the side" (Shanghai Theatrical College 1986: 217). De'ang women are described and illustrated as wearing black turbans with colored wool balls at the ends, although photos also show some women wearing plain white headcloths. No mention is made of hoods. The photos show the women wearing rattan hoops and the authors comment: "to the De'angs, rattan hoops are a sign of beauty, without which a woman will be sneered at." Ignored in previous works, the account in the Shanghai Theatrical College volume, while not describing them, provides illustrations of De'ang shoulder bags.

Women's costumes are shown to include a white shoulder bag with thin red vertical stripes and small colored pompoms (p. 221, photo nos. 530 and 531).

Diran's picture book on the hill tribes of Burma, as was noted in the first chapter, is of use primarily for its color photos of Silver Palaung from the Kalaw and Keng Tung areas (1997: 73–4), with those of Keng Tung mistakenly identified as Golden Palaung. The photos are useful since they are of Palaung living in areas not discussed in previous writings of Palaung dress. The most notable difference with these Palaung is that the women do not wear the distinctive hoods, but rather wear colorful headdresses made of string and beads. The captions and text provide basic descriptions of the women's dress in the photos. There is a little new information provided. For example, Diran notes that Palaung women don "lacquered bamboo hoops round the waist when they are married" (72)—such hoops are often made of rattan rather than bamboo. He also reports that the headdresses of married and unmarried women vary, with unmarried women wearing embroidered black caps with numerous pompoms and married women wearing the string and bead headdresses (75). Our own fieldwork, which will be discussed below, indicates that these types of headgear are worn by Silver Palaung women, while the hoods mentioned by previous authors are identified with the Golden Palaung. In addition, it appears that the hoops are worn by Silver Palaung and not by Golden Palaung.

Another potential source of information on Palaung dress are museum collections. Unfortunately, Palaung textiles are almost completely absent from the major museum collections of Burmese hill tribe textiles (see Howard 1999). While the British collections tend to favor textiles from the more warlike tribes (many of the pieces were acquired by Colonel Green in the course of his recruiting for the Burma Rifles) and from the Shan with their princes, the American collections reflect the activities in Burma of Christian missionaries (mainly Baptists). The Palaung, being neither particularly warlike nor fertile ground for Christian missionaries, tended to be overlooked. Thus, there are no Palaung textiles in the important collections of Denison University (Granville, Ohio), the Pitt Rivers Museum (University of

Oxford), the American the Museum of Natural History (New York), or The Field Museum (Chicago). Nor are there any in the collection of The Ethnographical Museum of Göteborg, Sweden, which houses a relatively good collection of textiles acquired by Ebba and René Malaise during a trip through the Shan states in 1934 (Hansen 1960). The Malaises visited twelve tribes in the Shan states, but not the Palaung. The Bankfield Museum in Halifax, United Kingdom, houses one of the most important collections of Burmese hill tribe textiles. The earlier pieces acquired by the museum (see Start 1917) do not include Palaung textiles, but in 1955 the museum did acquire a group of eighteen Palaung textiles. While the place of origin of the pieces is not given, most of them are identified by clan: Maningkwim (skirt, jacket, kerchief, turban, gaiters), Yarbon (skirt, jacket, hood), Manton (skirt, jacket, hood, turban), Manyawn (turban, gaiters). Several of these pieces appear in color plates in Howard (1998: pls. 180–92).

SUB-GROUP DIFFERENCES

While most of the early surveys of tribal people in Burma provide brief descriptions of this dress, unfortunately, there are few details. In particular, although there are differences in female dress among sub-groups of Palaung, the existing literature is not much help in precisely identifying these differences. Moreover, Silver Palaung dress is ignored in virtually all of the published accounts (Diran being an exception).

Scott and Hardiman (1900: 487), possibly in reference to the Palaung in Tawngpeng state, comment that "it does not appear that the dress of the women, though it is distinct from that of the Shans and Kachins, keeps up the old clan distinctions." However, later reports seem to contradict this. Lewis (1919: 38), for instance, notes that "there are numerous sub-tribes or clans of Palaungs clearly distinguishable from each other in dress," without further detail. Milne (1910: 135), in her initial study of the Shan, states that "the clan to which they [the Palaung] belong may be known by the width and colour of the stripes running horizontally round the dress." However, she gives no examples identifying skirts with clans. In her later (Milne 1924) monograph she elaborates a little:

> Excepting the skirt, the garments of the women of each Palaung or Palê clan are cut to the fashion of the clan, although they vary in colour and texture. The skirt (*klang*), however, is of the same straight shape for the women of all clans. The stuff of which it is made is woven in horizontal stripes, which, as in the Scottish tartans, vary in width and colour in the different clans. The stripes show to which clan a woman belongs—she would never dream of wearing a skirt woven with the stripes of any other clan but her own.

This said, she then fails to provide any further information about the particular patterns of each clan.

The Palaung textiles in the Bankfield Museum collection are more useful for our purposes in that, as was noted above, they come from four distinct clans: Maningkwim, Yarbon, Manton, and Manyawn. Unfortunately, no additional information accompanies the pieces to allow us to better understand sub-group differences in dress.

More recently, the Shanghai Theatrical College's survey of minority costumes in China remarks that the different groups within the De'ang nationality can be distinguished by the characteristics of their skirts and describes the distinctive skirts of three different groups: those referred to as the Red De'ang, Floral De'ang, and Black De'ang (1986: 216–21). The captions accompanying the photographs, however, generally do not identify the sub-group of the style of dress depicted. In addition, as usual, there is the problem of trying to ascertain what these Chinese designations mean in regard to the ethnic classifications in Burma. The women's costumes depicted in the photographs resemble, but are not precisely like, those worn by Palaung women in Burma. The skirt patterns and headcloths in particular are different from those found in Burma. Among the similarities are the style of blouse worn by Red and Floral De'ang and their shoulder bags.

3.5. "Rumai woman." From Milne (1924), facing p. 370.

Thus, from the above discussion, while it is apparent that significant differences in dress do exist among the various Palaung sub-groups, the existing literature is far from adequate for an understanding of these differences. The present work focuses on the Silver Palaung and below we will describe Silver Palaung dress. A more comprehensive depiction of the dress of the different Palaung sub-groups will have to await future research.

SILVER PALAUNG DRESS

Our data on Silver Palaung dress comes from our fieldwork in Thailand and the Kalaw area in Burma, as well as an examination of photographs and items of dress from Silver Palaung living in the Keng Tung area. Comparison of the three areas indicates no significant differences in female attire from one area to the other. Likewise, the terms used for items of dress seem to be identical for the most part.

With the exception of Diran, previous published works have little to say about Silver Palaung dress (usually referred to as the Pale) and the data generally comes from the Tawngpeng area. As mentioned above, Scott and Hardiman (1900: 487) describe the dress of Pale women as comprised of "a hood which is entirely white, with a short dark-blue coat and a skirt striped horizontally with red and blue." Milne (1924: 18, fn. 2) adds that the Golden Palaung do not generally wear cane girdles as do the Silver Palaung or Pale. This being the case (and for other reasons), it would appear that the Golden Palaung (or Shwe) living near Keng Tung described by Diran (1997) are in fact Silver Palaung as are those he encountered in the vicinity of Kalaw. Unfortunately, since we have not been able to visit Palaung communities near Keng Tung, we have not been able to confirm this belief.

Silver Palaung women weave on a backstrap loom and weaving usually takes place either under the house or on the front porch. Neither the Palaung of Kalaw nor those of northern Thailand make their own thread any longer. Rather, they purchase commercial thread or yarn from nearby markets (e.g., in Kalaw or Chiang Dao). When the Silver

3.6. Silver Palaung woman in Pang Daeng Nai modeling a type of headcloth *(kamai)* from Burma that is no longer worn in Thailand (Mar. 1998)

Palaung now living in northern Thailand lived in Burma they planted cotton and hemp (*kateim*) and made their own thread. Cotton was used for clothing and personal shoulder bags and hemp for rice bags and other heavy bags. In Burma natural dyes are still sometimes used. In particular, the dominant red color for the tubeskirts is often made from the root of a local tree. Increasingly, however, commercial dyes are used, often in the form of pre-dyed thread. Silver Palaung women in Thailand no longer use natural dyes, although they sometimes did before coming to Thailand. Now they tend to use pre-dyed thread. Prior to coming to Thailand the back support of the loom was made of leather, but in Thailand now it is made from plastic rice bags—and women complain that this makes their backs sore since it is less elastic. One other difference is that in Burma weaving and clothing production is seasonal, but in Thailand women weave year-round. This reflects changes in the overall economic adaptation and especially reduced opportunities for agricultural work in Thailand (such as tea growing and pickling).

In Burma weaving and the production of clothing is for domestic use and not for sale, although in the Kalaw area textiles are occasionally sold to visitors and Burmese traders have bought up most of the older pieces (especially the headcloths which are not often worn any more). In Thailand weaving and the production of clothing is also primarily for domestic use as well, but because of the presence of a much larger tourist industry and limited agricultural opportunities, some effort has been made to sell textiles to tourists. As will be discussed in the final chapter, however, these efforts have not been very successful.

The Silver Palaung woman's blouse is referred to as a *salow*. Blouses in both Burma and Thailand are commonly made of a variety of commercial fabrics with a preference for shiny fabrics. It is rare to see blouses made from hand-woven fabric. The blouses open down the center of the front without buttons or ties. They are relatively short and have long sleeves. There is a tendency for younger women to wear blouses of brighter colors (light blue is popular) and for older women to wear black blouses. The center opening and collar are edged with a wide piece of red cloth that is decorated in a variety of ways. It is often edged with thin pieces of cloth in white, yellow, or other colors. The bottom of the blouse and the sleeves may also be decorated with thin

3.7. Silver Palaung woman wearing a *kamai* (headcloth)

strips of cloth and straight or zig-zag lines of stitching in various colors. Additional decoration in the form of sequins, metal disks, and strands of brightly colored yarn are also commonly attached along the edges and seams of the blouse. Younger women's blouses generally are more decorative, but the black blouses of older women may be heavily decorated as well. Using two blouses from Pang Daeng Nai by way of example, the body of one measures 67 cms across the bottom with a height at the center of 39 cms and the body of the other measures 70 x 41 cms. The sleeves of the first blouse are 30 cms long and 15 cms wide and those of the second 30 x 16 cms. In comparison, the body of a blouse from the Kalaw area measures 43 x 36 cms and its sleeves 40 x 15 cms. Thus, its body is narrower than those from Pang Daeng Nai.

The tubeskirt worn by Silver Palaung women is called *glahng*, with the "ng" sound almost silent. Unlike the blouses, the tubeskirts are still always made from hand-woven cotton cloth (using commercial cotton thread). The tubeskirt is made from three pieces of cloth sewn together with no separate hem piece or waistband. The pieces are stitched together with white thread. While some Palaung sub-groups add bands of decorative embroidery to their skirts, among the Silver Palaung decoration is limited to various widths and colors of plain horizontal stripes. The bulk of the skirt is red, with very thin horizontal lines in different colors (commonly blue, green, and yellow) roughly evenly spaced throughout the body, and bands at each end. These bands are either mostly plain yellow or feature numerous thin stripes in various colors. To some extent among the Silver Palaung in Thailand, skirts with the plain yellow bands are favored by older married women and those with multi-colored thin stripes by younger women, but there is no hard and fast rule about this. From a sample of Silver Palaung tubeskirts from Thailand, the Keng Tung area, and the Kalaw area, there is no significant difference in the dimensions of the skirts on the basis of region. They range in width from 60 cms to 68 cms and from 101 cms to 110 cms in length.

In Burma Silver Palaung commonly wore leggings, called *kabajeng*, but these are not worn in northern Thailand. The leggings are made of plain black cotton and are tied with a piece of thread.

Silver Palaung women wear a variety of hoops and belts or sashes around their waists. It is the rattan and bamboo hoops in particular that Silver Palaung women point to as being the most important part of their dress signifying their Silver Palaungness. Neighboring peoples such as the Jingpho (who are also known as Kachin) also wear lacquered rattan hoops, but there are differences in the type of hoop and style of wearing them. Shila (1993) notes that the wearing of these rattan hoops by the Palaung is associated with an important origin legend. The legend tells that the angel Roi Ngoen came to earth, but was caught in a Lisu animal trap. The Silver Palaung believe that they are descendants of Roi Ngoen and wear the hoops, which represent the trap, to remind them of this. The hoops are also believed to protect the wearer and to bring good luck.

There are three types of hoop worn by Silver Palaung women: thin black lacquered hoops, 3 mm to 4 mm wide, referred to as *nong von;* wider bamboo or rattan hoops colored red with vertical stripes, ranging from 0.5 cm to 1 cm wide, called *nong rein;* and uncolored (referred to as "white") bamboo or rattan hoops decorated with small black circles, about the same width as the red hoops, called *nong doan.* The diameters of these hoops vary and are adjustable, depending on a person's size and taste. There is a general tendency for younger women to wear more hoops than older women. In addition, Silver Palaung women commonly wear a wide metal belt called a *nong rurh.* In the past these were made of silver, but now they are made of aluminum or some other similarly colored inexpensive metal. Women also wrap a plain white cotton sash around their waist, which is called a *nong roh.* Younger women in Pang Daeng Nai still make the hoops from locally available materials. They have the metal belts made for them in nearby Chiang Dao.

The type of headgear worn by Silver Palaung women poses an interesting problem. The existing early twentieth-century literature based on data from Tawngpeng indicates that Silver Palaung women there wear hoods (white ones), but today such hoods are not worn by Silver Palaung women in eastern and southern Shan State or in northern Thailand. Moreover, when questioned about the matter, older Silver Palaung were quite insistent that they had never worn hoods. Until it is possible to conduct further research on the matter in Tawngpeng and perhaps other areas in Shan State it is impossible to resolve this problem.

Milne (1924: 209) notes that Golden Palaung women wear a "loosely fitting black velvet cap (*hmok*), usually adorned with silver ornaments of coiled wire (*hma-e*)" under their hood. Decorated velvet caps are worn by Silver Palaung in the Kalaw and Keng Tung areas, but only by younger unmarried girls and women. They are not worn any longer by Silver Palaung in Thailand. Married Silver Palaung women in eastern and southern Shan State in the past wore a type of headcloth referred to as a *kamai* or *kamai gop*. These are not worn very often in Burma any longer and are not worn at all in Thailand, where they have been replaced by commercial towels. The kamai is a relatively involved piece of adornment. The center is usually made of plain white or black cotton cloth about one and a half meters in length. At each end of this are attached pieces of decorative cloth, each 20 cms to 30 cms in length. Long ago pieces of skirt material were used, but later it became common to use commercial cloth. The latter might be plain (blue, green, etc.) or patterned. The cloth is folded over one or two times depending on the width and sometimes stitched together at a few points. When folded the cloth is usually about 8 cms wide. Sequins are occasionally added to one side of the cloth for decoration. At each end of the cloth portion there are long strands of yellow and red string (and sometimes green) with Job's tears added. The strings are knotted in net-like fashion over a basket turned upside down. Occasionally the strings are simply left loose. These tassels range in length from 140 cms to 180 cms. The kamai is then wrapped around the head. Informants near Kalaw stated that a very long time ago women wore a very long headcloth, about ten meters, but that later it became fashion to wear a shorter one. Older women, usually widows, who practice the precepts of Buddhism and stay in the temple to sleep, do not wear a kamai, but replace it with a plain black headcloth. This is still practiced in northern Thailand.

An item called a *suk* is fastened around the kamai. The suk consists of a thin piece of cotton cloth (usually black) around which is wrapped silver or nickel wire. The suk appears to be similar to the coiled wire ornament mentioned by Milne. Women also wear additional items of jewelry. The Palaung generally do not make such jewelry themselves, but obtain it from traders or at local markets. This jewelry includes bead necklaces, bracelets (*kan dae*), and earrings (*blae heow*). Some of these are made by other ethnic minorities and in general they are not specific in their design to the Palaung.

Finally, both Palaung women and men carry shoulder bags made of hand-woven cotton cloth. The most common variety is called a *who*. It usually has a red ground with thin green and white vertical stripes and yellow and black stripes along the edges. There are also shoulder bags that have more decoration and tend to be slightly larger. They are often presented as gifts. Those referred to as *who nang* are given by a mother to her son, who in turn gives it to his girlfriend. One style of these decorative bags has a white ground with thin red vertical lines. On the sides there are thin red horizontal lines in groups of three and strands of variously colored thread attached as decoration. Another has a red ground, but its stripes are a little different from those on the more common type: there are variously colored vertical stripes as well as horizontal ones in groups of three. This type of bag also has strands of colored yarn attached as decoration.

When she marries, a Silver Palaung woman makes extra fancy blouses and skirts to wear and also presents a new set of clothing to her husband's parents. It is also common practice for the dead to be dressed in new clothing. The only specialized clothing is that worn by male shamans (curers). They wear black trousers and a black shirt.

CHAPTER 4

FLIGHT FROM BURMA

Unstable conditions in Burma over the past several decades have resulted in large numbers of members of minority groups fleeing across the border into Thailand. These include Karen, Lisu, Lahu, and Akha who have settled along the border area throughout northern Thailand. All of these refugees joined fellow members of their ethnic groups already living in Thailand. In the case of the Karen, they had lived in the border area for centuries. The other groups had migrated into Thai territory first during the late nineteenth and early twentieth centuries: the Lahu since the 1880s, the Akha and Lisu since around 1900. This movement had its origins to some extent in an earlier period of upheaval, originating in Yunnan, that had driven many hill tribe peoples south into British Burma. Some Palaung, as mentioned earlier, were among those fleeing into the relative security of British territory. They did not, however, at this time move any farther southeast into what is now Thailand. This movement only came much later and when the Silver Palaung fled to Thailand in the early 1980s they were the first Palaung to move into Thai territory.

The Silver Palaung presently living in northern Thailand previously resided across the border in Burma in the hills of southeastern Shan State. They came from a group of six villages (Nalang, Makuntok, Huay Tum, Huay Tum Long, Nam Hu Song Ta, and Pang Yong) on the slopes of Loi Lae (Doi Lae or Lae Mountain) located east of the Nam Taeng (or Namhtan) River about six hours' walk from the town of Keng Taung, west of the Salween River, and north of the town of Muang

Pan. They referred to themselves as Dara-ang or "close to the mountain."

The Silver Palaung of Loi Lae grew tea and beans for sale and rice and other crops for subsistence. Their reputation was that of peaceful tea growers who had cordial relations with others, but who kept pretty much to themselves. They also produced some opium to fulfill tribute requirements. When we were discussing the role of the village headman with Kam-hieng once, he commented that one of the most difficult aspects of being headman back in Burma had been the responsibility for meeting the opium tribute requirements. The headman would be given orders annually as to how much opium was to be collected in the village and he was then accountable to see to it that the opium was delivered safely and in the amount required. Failure to do so would result in punishment for the headman.

Prior to Burmese independence from Britain, these Silver Palaung had been under the chaofa of Muang Nai, but, as with most Palaung, matters relating to politics and administration mainly took place at the village level. External relations were limited. Outsiders almost never visited and trips by Palaung very far beyond their village were rare. The annual tribute payment was one of the few instances where external authority intruded on village life. External commercial relations were somewhat more important. Pickled tea, beans, and other crops were sold at nearby markets or to itinerant traders. Only a very limited range of goods was purchased from outside sources. People sometimes would leave their village on religious pilgrimages, although most religious affairs were also conducted within the village.

The Second World War brought some changes to Shan State, as the Japanese occupied some towns and as Muang Pan and Keng Tung State came under Siamese control. By and large, however, the violence associated with the war appears to have been of more relevance to the Shan and some of the other ethnic groups than to the Palaung, especially the Silver Palaung, who did their best to stay out of the way.

The political and military chaos and related economic changes of postwar Shan State initially had less of an impact on the Silver Palaung of southern Shan State than on peoples in other parts of the state. Increased opium production was the first major change. Opium tribute had been an important source of revenue for the Shan chaofa prior to British efforts to suppress opium production starting with the 1923 Shan States Opium Act (McCoy, Read, and Adams 1972: 72). The Silver Palaung, however, were minor suppliers of opium compared to other groups. This situation began to change after the Kuomintang (KMT) troops of General Li Mi overran Keng Tung State in the early 1950s. Li Mi's forces required all hill tribe farmers in the state to pay an annual opium tax that led to increased production in some villages and to the introduction of opium production in others. It was from this time that the payment of the opium tribute or tax became a significant burden to many Silver Palaung.

The early military disturbances in Shan State were not directly relevant to the Silver Palaung. Nor were they of much relevance to other Palaung. The Pa-o Karen uprising by the Karen National Defence Organization in the late 1940s and early 1950s took place in Yawng Hwe and Muang Nai states to the southwest of Keng Tung. Palaung living in the vicinity appear to have remained out of the way of most of the conflict surrounding this rebellion. The area around Loi Lae was apparently free of violence.

The situation began to change in the early 1960s, when more widespread conflict broke out in Shan State following General Ne Win's 1962 coup. Many Palaung communities in Shan State were badly affected by the armed conflict that took place from the 1960s until the 1992 cease-fire. The Shan uprising of 1959 began in northern Shan State. Later, the Shan National Independence Army was active in Yawng Hwe and Muang Nai states. During the early and mid-1960s Shan National Independence Army forces became active in the area between the Nam Taeng and Salween rivers (see Yawnghwe 1987: 125). Although the Silver Palaung generally managed to avoid the fighting, it was coming closer. The initial activities of the Chinese-backed Communist Party of Burma took place mainly in northeastern Shan State in Wa territory and away from areas occupied by the Palaung. In the early 1970s, however, the Communist Party of Burma established forward areas around Muang Nai and along the Nam Taeng River. In addition, in the early 1980s the Thailand Revolutionary Army (merged forces of the Shan United Revolutionary Army and an anti-communist faction of the Shan State Army) became active around Muang Pan in the region between the Nam Taeng and Salween rivers. The fighting was now uncomfortably close to Loi Lae and it was not long before the villages of Loi Lae found themselves drawn into a conflict which they had hoped to avoid.

Since they were not willing participants in the fighting in Shan State, the Silver Palaung have been pretty much ignored in accounts of the conflict. To the extent that attention has been paid to the Palaung, it has been the Golden Palaung of Namhsan who have been mentioned. This is because a small group of Golden Palaung there led by Kyaw Hla formed an insurgent group named the Palaung State Liberation Party (PSLP). Smith (1991: xiii) estimated the strength of the PSLP to be around 500 in 1989. The PSLP allied itself with larger opposition forces, including the National Democratic Front (which was formed in 1976), and gained control of a so-called liberated zone. Smith (1991: 96), comparing the situation in Burma with that in Northern Ireland, comments that "disparaging comments have been made, particularly in Rangoon, about the relatively small size of some of the ethnic armies . . ." However, "relatively small armed groups, such as the Palaung State Liberation Party, the KNPP and the (Muslim) Rohingya Patriotic Front, have had equally disturbing impacts in their own communities over the past few decades . . ." This has certainly been the case in Namhsan, where conflict between the PSLP and the Burmese armed forces disrupted the lives of most Palaung living in the area. It has also been the fate of the Silver Palaung of Loi Lae.

OPPRESSION AND THE FLIGHT FROM LOI LAE

During the 1970s and early 1980s the Silver Palaung of Loi Lae found themselves increasingly drawn into the fighting between the Burmese army and various rebel groups, primarily communist and Shan forces. The first serious trouble began when Communist Party of Burma forces arrived not only demanding food and shelter, but also young men from the villages to fight for them.

No one wanted to go with the communists, but it was apparent to village leaders that if there were no volunteers, the communists would cause trouble and take men away by force. When the communists came and demanded that his village provide four men, Kam-hieng, in his role as village headman, called a meeting to discuss the communist ultimatum. First he asked for volunteers to go for the sake of the safety of the village. Only a couple of men agreed but the communists wanted four men to serve with them for one year. Further discussions were held and finally the community members agreed that the community as a whole would look after the families of those who went and give them money as an added incentive. The money was to be raised within the village. After this, four men agreed to go. Kam-hieng made sure that those who went were good people who would stay with the communists for the whole year to ensure that the communists would not come back and cause further harm to the village.

The four young men left with the communists and the following year another four were sent to replace to original four, and so on. In addition, villagers were frequently pressed into serve to carry heavy loads of ammunition and other things, to build camps, and to carry messages. Some of those who were forced to fight with the communists and to work for them were killed or died from the harsh conditions. Burmese troops also destroyed houses and crops and raped Palaung women in reprisal for purported Palaung support of the communists.

To raise money to compensate the families of the men who were forced to fight with the communists, the villagers had to sell cattle, crops, and other things. This went on until the villagers had virtually nothing left to sell. Then the communists demanded that the men serve for three years instead of one, since one year was not long enough to properly train the men. Some men agreed to serve for three years, but the villagers knew that this was too much and that they could not continue to support the men's families. Weary of violence against them by Burmese forces and fearing eventual communist retribution, some families began to flee into the forest.

As a growing number of people deserted Loi Lae, in 1984 Kam-hieng and other leaders of the mountain villages decided that it was time for everyone to leave. The situation had become intolerable. They decided secretly to have everyone abandon their homes and to gather the remaining people near Wunsaria. The plan was to seek safety across the Salween River toward the border with Thailand. They remained near Wunsaria for three days and two nights as people gathered. The group comprised about seventy families. There were no animals since they had all been taken or sold.

The trip took about ten days. They took rice with them for food. Occasionally women were sent to ask Thai Yai for food and they were given fermented beans. They went along the road to Muang Pan (Mong Pan) and then crossed the Salween River to Muang Ton (Mongton). There were Burmese soldiers on one of the bridges. Kam-hieng says they showed the soldiers that they were suffering and told them that there was always fighting around the village and that they would cause no trouble. Otherwise they sought to cross rivers and pass check points at night and went through the forest after crossing the Salween River to the road east of Muang Ton.

The Palaung from Loi Lae temporarily settled near Muang Ton. The area around Muang Ton was outside of communist control, but it proved to be no sanctuary for the Palaung. They now found themselves in territory controlled by Khun Sa's Shan United Army. Palaung in this region were often forced to work as porters carrying drugs and other items for the Shan United Army and Khun Sa. Moreover, they found themselves caught in the crossfire of another conflict: that between Khun Sa's forces and the Burmese army.

Largely because of the unsettled conditions around Muang Ton, later in 1984, 168 Palaung from Loi Lae decided to cross the border into Thailand. They first settled immediately across the border at a site that came to be named No Lae. At this time there were no other Palaung living there. Nor were there any troops (Shan, Wa, Burmese, or Thai).

CHAPTER 5

LIFE IN NORTHERN THAILAND

No Lae was the first village established by the Palaung in Thailand. Subsequently they were to establish several more villages in Fang and Chiang Dao districts. In addition to No Lae, other Palaung villages in Fang District include Suan Cha and Mae Ram. The villages in Chiang Dao District include Pang Daeng Nai, Huai Pong, and Pang Daeng Nok. There are also a few Palaung living at Mae Chon. Our research has focused on Pang Daeng Nai and No Lae and these will receive the most attention in the present chapter.

Since 1984, additional Palaung have crossed over the border from Burma in search of sanctuary. Media attention focused on the Palaung briefly in January 1989 after a group of about 120 Palaung crossed into Thailand and thirty-four of them were arrested by Forestry officers and police in Chiang Dao District. They were charged with illegally entering Thailand and cutting down trees to make shelters. The old men, women, and children in the group remained free, while twenty-nine men eventually were put in jail and charged. They were sentenced to eleven years and five months imprisonment, but the sentence was later reduced to five years and nine months. A 1991 newspaper article commented on how those remaining free were suffering while the men remained in prison (*Siam Rath,* 5 February 2534).

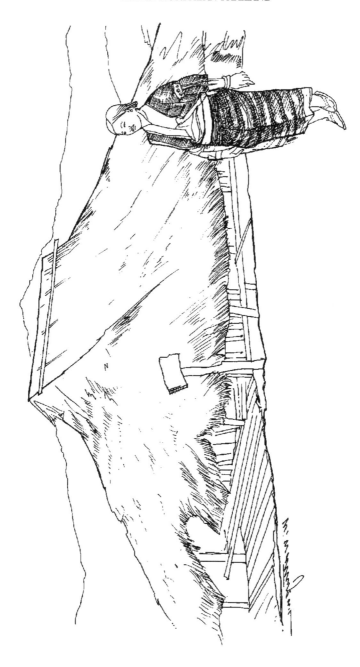

5.1. Woman and house at No Lae

NO LAE

The new settlement of No Lae was located near one of the Royal Hill Tribe Development and Welfare Projects located at Ang Khang. In December 1971 the Joint United Nations–Thai Programme for Drug Abuse Control in Thailand signed an agreement, with the largest part of its budget earmarked for agricultural and community development, focusing on Blue Hmong, White Hmong, Lisu, Lahu, Karen, and Haw. Working in conjunction with the Royal Project on Hill Tribe Development and Welfare, the joint United Nations–Thai drug abuse project established a "highland development station at Ang Khan, to demonstrate the commercial viability of certain field crops, fruit, and livestock production" (Suwanbubpa 1976: 37–8, 47). As part of this project, Kasetsart University conducted research on fruit trees and upland crops at the Ang Khang Experimental Station.

During one of the king's visits to Ang Khang, while he was at the Lisu village of Ban Khop Dong, one of the Palaung managed to meet with the king. The Palaung man told the king about the troubles that the Palaung had faced in Burma and asked permission for them to remain at No Lae in Thailand. The king granted them permission to remain.

The Forestry Department allowed the Palaung to farm on 250 rai of land near their new village. They began to grow corn, rice, taro, and beans on this land. But this land was barely adequate to support the original migrants, and those Palaung who arrived later had no land at all. They were unable to earn a living from their traditional sources such as tea and beans. Some Palaung worked as laborers for nearby Thai, Shan, and Haw, planting corn, rice, and poppies.

In addition to economic problems, the Palaung soon found that they had not completely escaped from the conflicts of Burma. Khun Sa's forces appeared and forced some Palaung to work for them once again. More importantly, the Palaung soon found themselves caught in the middle of a fight between Khun Sa and rival Wa forces seeking to wrest control of the heroin trade from him. While the Palaung generally tried to stay out of the way, their sympathies appear to have been with the Wa. One informant told us that one evening the Wa came to them and

5.2. House at No Lae

asked where Khun Sa's army was located. They told the Wa, who then attacked Khun Sa's troops. In addition, a short time later Burmese soldiers attacked the Wa.

In an effort to assist the Palaung at No Lae, representatives from the royal project at Ang Khang visited the village in 1989 and told the people to plant fruit trees (peach, persimmon, and plum) on their 250 rai. The representatives told the villagers that this would allow them to earn considerably more money than was possible with the crops they were growing at the time. They also started planting flowers to sell to the royal project in 1994 and added strawberries in 1995. The trees began bearing fruit in 1998. Under the scheme, all of the best products must be sold to the royal project, while they themselves can sell the inferior products. These innovations have improved the economic situation of No Lae to some extent, but the limited amount of land available continues to be a problem, as does finding adequate supplies of water for the new crops. There are not enough pipes to carry water to the fields from potential sources and water is acutely short during the dry season. Such difficulties have motivated people to continue to migrate away from No Lae.

By 1998 No Lae had ninety-two households and 110 families. The total population was 486 (244 males and 242 females). The establishment of a small border outpost by Thai authorities next to No Lae has helped to reduce fighting in the immediate vicinity. The Burmese army has built a similar base on its side of the border. To help ease relations with the Burmese, the Thais began providing them with electricity. When tensions have arisen, the threat of cutting off the electricity has generally proven sufficient to calm things down again.

To some extent, No Lae village resembles Palaung villages in Burma. There are no long houses, but some of the houses are built in typical Palaung style with large front verandahs. There is no proper Buddhist temple; however, there is a place to house monks. The village has its shrine on the outskirts known as a *da mu muang*, where ceremonies are held twice a year. It has its "heart" (*huja rawl*) as well, located along the road passing through the center of the village. There is also a typical

Palaung site for cremations, the *parero.* In addition, most women continue to weave and to wear distinctive Palaung dress. Missing, of course, are the pits to pickle tea in.

To escape from the fighting and faced with a shortage of land around No Lae, some of the Palaung migrated away from the border area. In her survey of the Palaung, Shila (1993) counted six Palaung settlements in northern Thailand. In addition to No Lae, with an estimated 150 households, she mentions Suan Cha with 100 households and Mae Ram with 30 households also in Fang District, and Pang Daeng (now known as Pang Daeng Nai) with 12 households and Huai Pong with 12 households in Chiang Dao District. Those leaving No Lae first migrated to Mae Chon, where a few people had been working for a tea grower. Most Palaung subsequently left Mae Chon and moved to the vicinity of Chiang Dao in 1985.

PANG DAENG NAI

Since its founding in 1985 Pang Daeng Nai (which initially was known simply as Pang Daeng) has grown, and in 1997 it had forty households with a population of 210 people. The village is located on a parcel of ten rai that the people purchased from a Thai who claimed to own the land. As is common in Thailand, however, there was no formal title and ownership is somewhat ambiguous.

Pang Daeng Nai also resembles Palaung villages in Burma. Even more than in No Lae, the houses are built in typical Palaung fashion. Again, there are no long houses, although one house in Pang Daeng Nai is fairly long. The houses are made of wood and slit bamboo. They are raised from one to three meters off the ground and have a verandah in the front. Weaving, thatching, and a variety of other activities take place either on the verandah or underneath the house. The roof is thatched and the thatch is replaced every one to two years (occasionally after three years). Over the front door it is common to place a small protective emblem made of seven crossed layers of bamboo known as a *da laew.* Inside the door is a common room. To one side of this is located

5.3. Rear view of a house at Pang Daeng Nai (Mar. 1998)

the central house post. The hearth is often located near this post and may be in an area distinct from the common room. The hearth has three legs. This portion of the house is commonly divided by raising the floor slightly in the middle, in effect creating two rooms. Toward the back of this portion of the house there is a household shrine or *yang phra*. The other side of the house is often partitioned with a wall and functions as a bedroom for family members. In Burma the preference was to sleep with one's head toward water and one's feet toward the mountains. In the crowded conditions of Pang Daeng Nai this is not always possible.

A large *huja rawl* or village heart sits prominently in the center of the village. It has a bell that is used to call the people together whenever

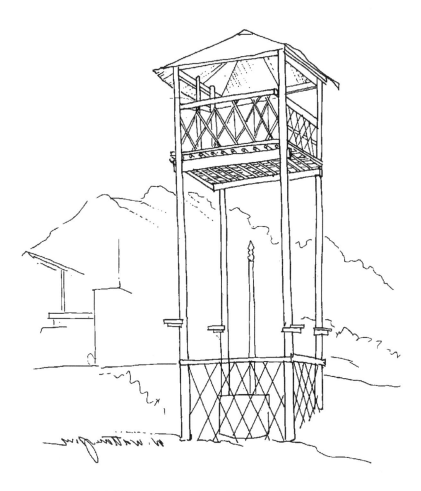

5.4. Village heart *(huja rawl)* of Pang Daeng Nai

the need arises. There is also a *da mu muang* shrine located in the forest above the village where the villagers go twice a year, at the commencement and end of Buddhist lent (in mid- to late July and mid-October to mid-November respectively), to give offerings to the village spirit known as the *chao muang*. The shrine is said to be closed during Buddhist lent and no one is allowed to marry during this time. Offerings are also made to the forest spirit. Within the village there is a priest or shaman (*dayan*) who is responsible for overseeing such ceremonies and for maintaining proper relations with these and other spirits. The shrine is also sometimes the site of offerings when an individual is ill. The sick person goes to the local curer who holds the patient's hands to determine what the person did or what was done to the person to cause the illness. The person then takes an offering to the village shrine or to a site in the forest associated with a particular spirit.

Although Pang Daeng Nai has its village shrine and village heart, it does not have a Buddhist temple. This in part reflects space constraints. Around 1997, however, the Palaung of Pang Daeng Nai joined others in nearby villages in supporting the construction of a nearby cave temple complex known as Wat Tham Phrabat. By 1999 this included a residence for monks and a long decorative stairway to the cave temple. Also, monks occasionally visit the village and the people of Pang Daeng Nai often attend important religious ceremonies at Chiang Dao.

Kam-hieng led those who settled at Pang Daeng Nai. As was mentioned earlier, he had been head of one of the villages on Loi Lae back in Burma. Prior to becoming a village headman he had been a monk for eight years. He was chosen to be head of the village through consensus at a meeting mainly of household heads. He had asked to be relieved of his duties on several occasions, but each time had been persuaded to remain the village head. During our visits to Pang Daeng Nai it became clear that Kam-hieng exerted considerable moral authority over the villagers and that he was viewed by them as being the one primarily responsible for protecting the village and for ensuring internal orderliness. He took his job seriously and strove to do his best to see to it that the village did the best it could in this new environment. Thus, he encouraged the people to work hard, to keep their village

5.5. Village shrine (*da mu muang*) of Pang Daeng Nai

clean, to keep out drugs, and to adopt family planning. The latter reflected the view that land was limited and steps needed to be taken to keep the population at a level that could be supported on the land available. This began with a ban on others moving into the village and then promotion of family planning.

Other people holding special positions in Pang Daeng Nai include the *hsa-ra* or male religious specialist who also engages in curing, and female midwives. There is one *hsa-ra* in the village. In fact, it is hard to imagine a Palaung village functioning without such a person. Older women usually function as midwives. Kam-hieng's mother, for example, is a midwife.

On the land adjacent to Pang Daeng Nai the villagers grow crops such as rice, beans, and corn. Two crops are planted each year, but only beans tend to grow well for the second planting. All three crops are grown to meet the bulk of people's subsistence needs, but they are also an important source of household income. Surplus crops generally are sold to middlemen who come to the village, rather than being taken to Chiang Dao to sell. Some families are unable to grow enough to eat for the entire year and must buy food, mainly rice, from outside the village. A few animals are kept in the village, mostly chickens. These are raised primarily for subsistence needs.

Agricultural productivity in Pang Daeng Nai since its founding has been relatively poor. Water is in short supply for agricultural and household needs and the nearby stream is dry much of the year. The water supply for the village has been improved as a result of metal water tanks being built with external assistance, but the situation for agriculture remains critical. In recent years the rice yield has been reduced even further by disease. The situation has been exacerbated as a result of the loss to the government of access to agricultural land suitable for growing rice. During the early years of settlement people pretty well planted wherever they pleased, but increasing government restrictions greatly reduced the amount of land available for farming. Moreover, most of the remaining land is not of good quality and is only appropriate for growing corn and beans. The corn yield has not been good either. An additional problem is that the corn must be harvested fairly early to allow beans to grow, at a time when the price

5.6. Elephants for tourists next to Pang Daeng Nai's village heart (Mar. 1998)

for corn is relatively low. People must also sell beans earlier than they would like when prices are still low since they are in need of cash and cannot wait for prices to improve. Moreover, while beans were a relatively good money earner in Burma, the market for them in Thailand is poor. Thus, since coming to Thailand the Palaung have lost two relatively lucrative markets that had been available to them in Burma: for pickled tea and for beans.

In addition to the sale of crops, villagers earn money as day laborers working for the owners of nearby orchards and fields or in construction. The pay for those working in agriculture is B80 per day for women and B90 per day for men. When agricultural production is poor more people tend to look for work outside of the village. This was the case in 1998 when adverse weather conditions drastically reduced the normal crop yield. In fact, such work has become an increasingly important source of income in recent years as the villagers have faced more and more problems with agriculture. When working near the village, people walk to the orchards and fields. For work farther away, trucks come to the village in the morning to pick people up and return them in the evening. Such work is largely seasonal. The villagers have not been able to go further in search of work since they do not have adequate papers to allow them to do so. In addition, insecurity about their status in Thailand makes them afraid to venture too far from the village.

Items not produced in the village are generally obtained from the town of Chiang Dao. Itinerant sellers also occasionally visit the village. A group of about four or five Palaung came to Pang Daeng Nai from Burma in 1997 and again in 1998 to sell goods (canned beef, salted fish, and dried cattle skins) from across the border. They obtain permission to cross the border from Burmese and Thai soldiers and then rent a truck on the Thai side of the border to visit the Palaung settlements in Thailand. Following their visit there was an outbreak of malaria in Pang Daeng Nai. The villagers believe that the traders brought the disease and so told them not to come again. Malaria had been a problem when the people first moved to Pang Daeng Nai, but after people were checked by health authorities and received medicine it had disappeared. Thus, they were concerned about its reoccurrence.

Such traders also are known to bring amphetamines and heroin, but the headman in Pang Daeng Nai is very strict about drugs and has been able to keep it out of the village. In the past a few people used opium, but this has been banned as well. Since coming to Thailand they no longer grow opium poppies. The headman and other village leaders know that drugs are a serious problem in many other northern villages and are very anxious to block the use or sale of drugs in Pang Daeng Nai.

The people of Pang Daeng Nai are aware of the importance of the tourist industry in northern Thailand and know that many hill tribe villages have earned a good deal of money from the industry. They too have sought to earn money from tourism, but with little success to date. Tourists come to Pang Daeng Nai from Chiang Mai mainly either as part of a day-long tour that includes visits to several other hill tribes in the vicinity or to take elephant rides. The elephant rides are organized out of Chiang Dao and usually start in Pang Daeng Nai and finish in Huai Pong, from where the tourists are taken by truck back to Chiang Dao. Efforts are made to sell the tourists soft drinks and beer as well as handicrafts. The latter include locally made skirts, shoulder bags, and children's hats as well as inexpensive jewelry obtained from other ethnic groups. Villagers tend to swarm about tourists in an effort to sell such items. However, handicraft sales are fairly limited since few people know about the Palaung and their products are not viewed as being as attractive as those produced by other hill tribe groups.

Two families built dormitories for tourists in order to encourage people to spend the night. The charge is B20 per person and meals and dances are also available for an additional charge. Traditional Palaung dances (*ngah*) are performed mainly at festivals by both men and women and generally revolve around a story or narrative. Many Palaung villages in Burma have one or more dance specialist, usually a male, who teaches young people to dance. There are no special costumes for the dances. The dances performed for the tourists in Pang Daeng Nai were relatively simple affairs, often only loosely based on tradition, of the type usually performed for tourists: a fairly basic shuffle performed mainly by young people who at some point ask the tourists to join in. At first a few people stayed, but the numbers soon dwindled. One family gave up and the other only has guests on rare occasions. By and large, the Palaung are not included in Chiang Mai tours that include trekking and overnight stays. In fact, few tour agencies even mention the Palaung in their lists of hill tribes visited.

Finding a suitable marriage partner in a community the size of Pang Daeng Nai is always a problem. In addition to matters of personal taste and finding another single person of roughly the same age, there are five family names among the Palaung of Pang Daeng Nai and one cannot marry a person with the same name. In the past, men and women from the same family of marriageable age faced restrictions in communication, but this is not such a common practice any longer. When it proves impossible to find a Palaung mate in Pang Daeng Nai, young people look to other Palaung communities in Thailand. Thus, several people in Pang Daeng Nai have married Palaung from No Lae. Spouses are not found in Burma.

There is also the possibility of marrying non-Palaung. During the early days of residence in Thailand this was not so likely and today it is still relatively rare. When marriage does take place outside of the ethnic group it is usually a case of a Palaung woman marrying a non-Palaung man. Palaung men almost never marry non-Palaung women. If a Palaung woman marries a non-Palaung man she generally leaves Pang Daeng Nai to reside in her husband's community. When she does so she also usually ceases to wear Palaung dress. Thus, if a Palaung woman marries a Lahu man, she moves into the Lahu community and adopts Lahu dress.

Once a young couple has decided to marry and their families are in agreement, there is a matter of settling on the appropriate compensation or bride-price. In Burma this generally involved a cash payment (said to be in "gold or silver"). In Pang Daeng Nai an amount in Thai baht is negotiated. A common settlement is around B4,000. The bride also is expected to give the groom's mother a new dress. She also makes a wedding trousseau for herself that includes an especially fancy blouse.

When discussing the possibility of elopement, informants made it quite clear that this was considered very bad form. Those we talked to were adamant that prospective young couples should do things the proper way, even though it took time and cost money. There did not appear to have been any recent incidents, but should a couple elope, when they returned the practice was for the community to decide on an appropriate punishment. This usually involved payment of a fine.

The newly married couple usually resides with the groom's family. Households tend to include extended families of up to three generations. After a time, the couple may move into their own house and establish a new household. When such a move does take place, the preference is to try to locate the new house near to the house of the husband's parents.

When a person dies, the deceased is clothed, wrapped in a blanket or sleeping mat, and placed in a coffin (*karlai*). Wealthier persons are wrapped in blankets, while poorer ones are wrapped in sleeping mats (*m'beaw*). Also placed in the coffin are items associated with the person's livelihood. In the case of a man these include seeds representing the various crops planted in the community, banana leaves, and farming tools. The coffin is first placed in the house of the deceased. Monks are invited in the afternoon to pray and members of the community visit the house to pay their respects. The length of time that the coffin remains on display depends in part on the wealth and status of the family since food must be provided to those who visit. The period can last up to three days. In Burma it was common practice to bury the deceased and only monks tended to be cremated. Thus, after being displayed in the house the coffin was taken to the graveyard (*barew*) and buried. In the case of older persons a hole was dug and the coffin was placed in a cavity lined with wood. There were no grave markers, but people generally knew where individuals had been buried. In Thailand, however, everyone is cremated.

The relative isolation of the people of Pang Daeng Nai from the surrounding society has lessened over the years. Language has been an important factor in this regard. When they arrived in Thailand most people spoke only Palaung and a few spoke Shan. Today a growing number of people are also fluent in Northern Thai or Central Thai. School attendance has been especially important as a factor of socialization for younger Palaung at Pang Daeng Nai. There is an elementary school about one kilometer from the village which is attended by all of the children of the appropriate age. At the school not only are the Palaung children exposed to Thai language and culture, but they also mix with children from other hill tribes, mainly Lahu and Karen. Television, which is an important acculturative influence in many hill tribe communities, has not been a factor so far in Pang Daeng Nai.

OTHER PALAUNG SETTLEMENTS IN CHIANG DAO

The second largest Palaung community in Chiang Dao District is Huai Pong. The founding of Huai Pong dates to approximately the same time as Pang Daeng Nai, the villagers also moving there from Mae Jon. It is located a few kilometers to the south of Pang Daeng Nai. By 1997 the village had grown to twenty-two households. The people have no document indicating ownership of the land, but they think of it as theirs. Most villagers have only a blue identity card that allows them to remain in Chiang Mai Province.

Huai Pong has more of a ramshackle appearance than Pang Daeng Nai, but the house styles and over-all village appearance remains identifiably Palaung. There is a smaller *huja rawl* than the one at Pang Daeng Nai and there is a village shrine located just outside the village for prayers to the *chao moeng* spirit and spirit of the forest. As with Pang Daeng Nai, there is no Buddhist temple. The children go to the same school as those of Pang Daeng Nai.

Economic life in Huai Pong is similar to that of Pang Daeng Nai. Those villagers who have access to land grow rice, corn, and beans. Some villagers lease land from others on which to grow crops. People also occasionally work in nearby fields and orchards. Huai Pong is the end-point for the usual elephant ride for tourists, and the villagers have built a place for tourists to rest and offer them soft drinks and beer for sale.

Starting in 1994 a new group of Palaung migrants left No Lae to settle near Pang Daeng Nai along the main road to Chiang Dao. They named their settlement Pang Daeng Nok ("outside" to distinguish it from the original Pang Daeng, which was designated "in"). This group

5.7. Huai Pong's village heart (Mar. 1998)

left the Fang District claiming that they had no land and that there was little work available for them. The land on which they settled in Chiang Dao District is owned by a Lisu man. The man told them that they could come and live on his land, but to do so they had to become Christians. They agreed and converted from Buddhism to Christianity. This is a rare event among Palaung. In Burma, while Christian missionaries had considerable success among some ethnic minorities, such as the Karen, among others they made little headway. The Palaung were one group that showed little inclination to convert, for the most part remaining staunchly Buddhist. At least some of the villagers claim to be happier as a result of conversion since they no longer see ghosts or spirits

The houses in the new village are, for the most part, poorly constructed. As a reflection of their being Christians, the village lacks a traditional village heart and village shrine. The people view theirs as a Christian community. Accordingly, in 1997 they began construction of a small Christian church, obtaining most of the building materials from the nearby forest. Denial of access to the forest by government officials later in the year, however, put a halt to construction of the church.

In early 1998 there were sixteen Palaung families living in Pang Daeng Nok, about one hundred people. Initially they grew corn and beans on land near the settlement. They also planted corn for the land owner and earned money tending nearby mango orchards as well as working as day laborers in more distant fields. For the latter, as in Pang Daeng Nai, they are transported by trucks. In addition, one young man in the village works for a Thai non-governmental organization concerned with wildlife protection and he and two others have begun a three-year Bible study program in Chiang Rai which they anticipate will lead to paid employment.

To date the village has no headman. One of the young men taking part in the Bible study program, however, sometimes functions as a spokesman.

In early 1998 all of the men of Pang Daeng Nok were arrested on a charge of land invasion on forest reserve land. On the 22 June, after three months in jail, they were released pending their trial. In the meantime, no crops were planted and the land formerly used for agriculture by the village is now closed to them by Thai forestry officials. The community found itself completely dependent on a Christian church organization in Fang for food and facing a bleak future. When discussing the situation of the Palaung of Pang Daeng Nok with neighboring Palaung at Pang Daeng Nai, the latter expressed concern and pity for the former, but saw little that they could do to help since they too were facing reduced circumstances as a result of the loss of farm land. We will discuss the events of 1998 in more detail in the next chapter. Once again the Palaung found themselves caught in the midst of a battle between opposing forces.

CHAPTER 6

CONFLICTS IN NORTHERN THAILAND

Since 1998 the Palaung in Chiang Dao have found themselves increasingly drawn into conflicts involving questions about the rights and status of hill tribe peoples in northern Thailand. While perhaps not as life threatening as the conflicts they fled from in Burma, these are nevertheless serious matters that have implications for the future security and welfare of these Palaung communities. The conflicts in question revolve around two main issues: 1) that of Thai citizenship for hill tribe people and 2) land use or land management by hill tribe peoples living in or adjacent to various types of designated forest reserve lands. These are not new issues, but reforms emanating from the new Thai constitution have exacerbated tensions as various conservative forces have resisted them while others have pursued sometimes contradictory reform agendas.

The citizenship issue is a long-standing one for the hill tribe people living in northern Thailand and, while some progress has been made in resolving the issue in recent years, many problems remain. At present there are estimated to be between 200,000 and 300,000 hill tribe people holding a blue highlander identification card that allows them to reside in a particular area in northern Thailand, but places numerous restrictions on their residence, movement, employment, ability to own property, and other aspects of their lives. In addition, there are an unknown number of hill tribe people in northern Thailand without even this status. Obtaining the so-called blue cards is a relatively slow process and one that often entangles the applicant in corrupt practices by government officials. Most Palaung now living in northern Thailand presently have such blue cards. Having lived in Thailand now for some fifteen years and with little prospect of returning to Burma, these Palaung, along with most other blue card holders, would like to be granted citizenship.

The land issue centers around concern over utilization of the remaining forest land in northern Thailand and what is to be done with hill tribe people living in or using this land. The pro–hill tribe position favors the adaptation of so-called community forestry practices (see Ganjanapan 1992) which allow for the management of forest land by hill tribe peoples, who are viewed as guardians of the forest rather than its destroyers. Opposed to his position are a disparate array of interest groups. One of these includes environmentalist extremists who oppose any further use of the forest land and want all people removed from the forests. Another favors continued exploitation of at least some forest land, but also favors removal of hill tribes from the forests, or at least greater restrictions on them. This group argues that traditional hill tribe agricultural practices (especially slash-and-burn or swidden agriculture) play a major role in degrading the forests. Finally, there are those who want the hill tribes out of the way largely to allow their own unfettered exploitation of the forest, although their rationale for restricting hill tribe access to the forests is usually put in more moderate terms.

For the Palaung of Chiang Dao, the land issue became a serious concern after the deputy agriculture minister, Newin Chidchob, visited the north to inspect an area damaged by wildfire on 20 March 1998. Following his visit there was a crackdown on hill tribe people clearing land for farming in protected forest areas. The deputy minister ordered the governor of Chiang Mai Province to arrest hill tribe people in the area he visited near Chiang Dao who were encroaching on forest reserve land. Some critics argued that this was a cynical attempt to divert attention away from a scandal about illegal logging near the border with Burma involving influential people, but it also can be seen as an attempt by the national government to enforce legislation aimed at affording greater protection to forest lands. Whatever the reason behind the act, a group of fifty-six Palaung, Lahu, and Lisu men from Pang Daeng Nai and neighboring communities were arrested for illegally cutting trees and burning forest in a protected area and thereby violating the national

6.1. Woman and child at Pang Daeng Nai

forestry laws. Twenty-six of the fifty-six arrested were Palaung.

The impact on Pang Daeng Nai and Pang Daeng Nok was devastating. The families of the arrested men found themselves without food and deprived of a source of income. Moreover, the futures of both communities became uncertain since it looked as if they would have virtually no land on which to grow crops. Several non-governmental organizations involved in hill tribe affairs rallied to the defense of those arrested and their communities. Hill tribe advocates based at Chiang Mai University collected donations of food and money to help the families of those arrested and also raised money for the court case. Among those involved was the Ethnic Studies Network (ETHNET), formerly the Center for Ethnic Studies and Development, associated with the Regional Center for Social Sciences and Sustainable Development of Chiang Mai University and under the directorship of Dr. Chayan Vaddhanaphuti. The involvement of Chiang Mai University faculty in support of the hill tribes became a focal point of the ire of those wishing to remove the hill tribes from the area and effigies of three of the academics (Chayan Vaddhanaphuti, Anan Ganjanapan, and Shalardchai Ramitanond) were burned in public. Kam-hieng emerged as a spokesman for the Palaung and the others arrested and was interviewed by reporters on several occasions.

Finally, most of the men who had been arrested were freed on 22 June, after three months in jail, pending the outcome of their trial. Two Palaung men remained in jail since they did not have blue identity cards (they were ill the day Thai authorities came to issue the cards). Around the same time, the government began to soften its stance concerning land use and took steps to work out a compromise. Government officials conducted a survey to ascertain what land had been used over the past several years by the villagers for agriculture and eventually it was decided to allow the people of Pang Daeng Nai to continue to use some of the land on which they had farmed in the past. However, as was noted in the last chapter, the amount of land made available to them was a good deal less than what they had used in the past and was generally not suitable for rice cultivation. The case of Pang Daeng Nok was more serious since they had been settled in the area for only a short time and could make no claim that they had used the land for a sufficient length of time. They ended up being deprived of virtually all of their agricultural land. After numerous delays, in mid-1999 the court case finally ended with no Palaung being convicted and none remaining in jail. The few Palaung who had not been freed in June 1998 initially were put on probation, but since they had already served time in jail the court decided to drop the charges against them as well.

The arrests and subsequent loss of agricultural land has drawn the Palaung out of their isolation to an unprecedented degree. For one thing, it has forced the Palaung to think more seriously about finding other means of supporting themselves, often by working away from the communities. The arrests and campaign on their behalf also served to involve the Palaung politically with advocates for greater rights for hill tribes. Thus, when the director-general of the Royal Forestry Department invited the Palaung of Pang Daeng Nai to come to Chiang Dao to give a cultural performance at the amphoe (district) office during his visit on 28–29 December 1998, NGO activists urged the Palaung to use this as an opportunity to present him with the problems facing their village, especially problems related to identity cards. Such involvement in the political sphere is uncommon for Palaung, who, as we have seen, have a long history of seeking to avoid being drawn into conflicts. Most Palaung in Thailand continue to try to avoid potential conflicts and political involvement.

The Palaung of Chiang Dao were asked to participate in a large demonstration to be held in Chiang Mai that was sponsored by the Northern Farmers Network, the Assembly of Thai Ethnic Minorities, and the Assembly of the Poor. The demonstrations began on 25 April 1999 in front of the city hall and continued for several weeks. Thousands of participants took part, including members of seven minority groups, coming from an estimated 300 villages in eight of Thailand's northern provinces. Only a few Palaung participated, while most Palaung preferred to maintain a low profile in the hope of avoiding further trouble for themselves and their communities.

While Palaung involvement in the demonstration was limited, the issues were of direct relevance to their status and economic well-being in Thailand since the demonstrators were demanding enactment of legislation to promote community management of forest lands, accelerated granting of Thai citizenship, and more effort to resolve conflicts between minorities and government agencies. In regard to the land issue, the demonstrators felt that the four existing forest laws and regulations as well as various forest-related cabinet decisions needed reform to be in accordance with the new constitution which recognizes the right of individuals to participate in resource management and protection as well as the role of communities in conserving and managing the environment.

Initially the government was suspicious that the demonstration was being backed by opposition politicians. Finally, however, in early May government representatives undertook to negotiate with the demonstrators. On 9 May, an agreement was reached with three government representatives (Newin Chidchob, Plodprasob Suraswadee, and Amnuay Patise) on a number of issues. It was agreed that hill tribe people would register at district offices and be classified according to whether they held Thai citizenship or highland identification cards or were in the country illegally. Later the hill tribe people are to declare the forest land that they have been using so that a committee can establish whether their land claims are valid. If they are determined to be valid, a kind of certificate will be issued. If the claims are not deemed to be valid, then the land will be reclaimed by the Royal Forestry Department. It was further agreed that during implementation of these steps, no arrests would take place and people would be allowed to farm the land that they customarily have been farming. Finally, it was agreed that the government would organize a public hearing on the drafts of community forest bill (the draft at the time did not allow community forest in the protected forest areas) and pass the bill as soon as possible.

To the disappointment of the demonstrators, the memorandum of agreement based on the negotiations that was issued by the cabinet on 11 May included what they considered to be some crucial changes. In particular, the cabinet decided to grant a temporary arrest waiver only for those with Thai citizenship (thus excluding the Palaung). The leaders of the demonstration decided therefore to continue their protest in front of Chiang Mai city hall. Further informal negotiations made some progress in resolving outstanding issues and the organizers agreed to end the demonstration on 19 May.

During the course of the demonstration, those opposed to the aims of the demonstrators had actively campaigned against them. In particular, they had sought to stir up anti-hill tribe nationalistic feelings. Thus, the night before the demonstration was to end, it was learned by leaders of the demonstration that opponents planned to use force to break up the demonstration in the morning before the government representative arrived on the scene. One leader of the demonstration reports what happened next as follows:

> Signal rockets were fired above our heads and we were told that about 400 men with two fire engines were waiting behind the city hall. We must move out at dawn or else the police by the order of the governor would move in. We decided to avoid clashing with the police or another group of unidentified men, because there were women, old and sick people among us. So we decided to move out from the city hall. I asked the Police Commissioner in charge to give me 25–30 minutes before he ordered his men to clear the demonstration. Before I could tell our people to prepare to move out, around 1,000 RFD [Royal Forestry Department] officials and employees marched to the scene and confronted the demonstrators. Around 5:30 AM, some 500 policemen marched in between the RFD people and us, and at 6:15 the villagers began to leave the city hall. They walked slowly to Chiang Mai University; some were in tears, some looked frightened and in despair. No one understood why such a dispersement was necessary when both sides had already reached an agreement. It was clearly a violation of the new constitution of the Kingdom and of basic human rights.

The demonstrators gathered on the university campus at the former site of the Social Research Institute, which for years had been active in hill tribe affairs. The demonstrators dispersed once and for all on the afternoon of 21 May, feeling that they had made some progress in getting the government to meet their demands, but also concerned about future opposition in light of how the demonstration had ended.

As an epilogue, on 24 May opponents of the hill tribes known as the "Chom Thong group" presented the governor of Chiang Mai with flowers for the way in which he had dispersed the hill tribe demonstrators. They then moved on to the Chiang Mai University campus to protest the involvement of seven members of its faculty in the demonstration and demanded that disciplinary action be taken against them. Banners condemning "Mr. Chayan and his company" were hung from the Faculty of Social Science building. Two days later, on 26 May, the opposition arranged for a group of allied village and sub-district headmen to come yet again to present flowers to the governor and congratulate him for his actions. As they had the year before, members of this group also burned effigies of three prominent hill tribe advocates at Chiang Mai University (Chayan Vaddhanaphuti, Anan Ganjanapan, and Shalardchai Ramitanond).

The above events (as well as subsequent anonymous death threats issued against a couple of prominent advocates for hill tribe rights) indicate that the political fight for hill tribe rights in northern Thailand is far from over and could turn violent. Nevertheless, it is clear that progress has been made in resolving the land and citizenship issues. While the Palaung were not major participants in the campaign, their situation continues to bring attention to these issues. Whatever the outcome, it will have important implications for the Palaung in Thailand.

REFERENCES

Cameron, A. A. 1912. A Note on the Palaungs of the Kodaung Hill Tracts of Momeik State." Appendix A in *Census of India,* 1911, vol. 9, part 1, pp. i–xlii.

Chazee, Laurent. 1995. *Atlas des Ethnies et des Sous-Ethnies du Laos.* Bangkok: privately printed.

Dani, Ahmad H. 1960. *Prehistoric and Protohistoric of Eastern India: with a Detailed Account of the Neolithic Cultures in Mainland Southeast Asia.* Calcutta: Firma K. L. Mukhopadhyay.

Davies, H. R. 1909. *Yünnan: The Link Between India and the Yangtze.* Cambridge: Cambridge University Press.

Diffloth, G. 1991. Austro-Asiatic Languages. In *Encyclopaedia Britannica Macropaedia,* vol. 22, pp. 19–21.

Diran, Richard K. 1997. *The Vanishing Tribes of Burma.* London: Weidenfeld & Nicolson.

Fraser-Lu, Sylvia. 1988. *Hand-woven Textiles of South-East Asia.* Singapore: Oxford University Press.

Ganjanapan, Anan. 1992. Community Forestry Management in Northern Thailand. In *Regional Development and Change in Southeast Asia in the 1990s,* edited by A. Pongsapich, M. C. Howard, and J. Amyot, pp. 75–84. Bangkok: Social Research Institute, Chulalongkorn University.

Grimes, Barbara F., ed. 1992. *Ethnologue: Languages of the World.* 12th ed. Dallas, Texas: Summer Institute of Linguistics.

———. 1999. *Ethnologue: Languages of the World.* 13th ed. Dallas, Texas: Summer Institute of Linguistics.

Hansen, Henny Harald. 1960. *Some Costumes of Highland Burma at the Ethnographical Museum of Gothenburg.* Göteborg: The Ethnographical Museum.

Howard, Michael C. 1994. *Textiles of Southeast Asia: An Annotated & Illustrated Bibliography.* Bangkok: White Lotus.

———. 1999. *Textiles of the Hill Tribes of Burma.* Bangkok: White Lotus.

Kunstadter, Peter, Roger Harmon, and Sally Kunstadter. 1978. *Lua' of North Thailand: The Material Culture of the Upland Village of Pa Pae.* Seattle: Thomas Burke Memorial Washington State Museum, University of Washington.

Leach, E. R. 1954. *Political Systems of Highland Burma.* Cambridge, Mass.: Harvard University Press.

Lebar, Frank M., Gerald C. Hickey, and John K. Musgrave. 1964. *Ethnic Groups of Mainland Southeast Asia.* New Haven, Conn.: Human Relations Area Files.

Lowis, Cecil C. 1906. *A Note on the Palaung of Hsipaw and Tawngpeng.* Ethnographical Survey of India, Burma, Number 1. Rangoon: Superintendent of Government Printing and Stationery.

———. 1919. *The Tribes of Burma.* Rangoon: Superintendent, Government Printing.

Mangrai, Sao Saimong. 1965. *The Shan States and the British Annexation.* Data Paper Number 57, Southeast Asia Program, Department of Asian Studies, Cornell University, Ithaca, New York.

McKinnon, John, and Wanat Bhruksasri, eds. 1983. *Highlanders of Thailand.* Singapore: Oxford University Press.

McCoy, Alfred, Cathleen B. Read, and Leonard P. Adams II. 1972. *The Politics of Heroin in Southeast Asia.* New York: Harper & Row.

Milne, Leslie. 1910. *Shans at Home.* London: John Murray.

———. 1921. *An Elementary Palaung Grammar.* Oxford: Clarendon Press.

———. 1924. *The Home of an Eastern Clan: A Study of the Palaungs of the Shan States.* Oxford: Clarendon Press.

Reid, L. A. 1993. Morphological Evidence for Austric. *Oceania Linguistics,* vol. 33, pp. 323–44.

Scott, James George. 1921. *Burma: A Handbook of Practical Information.* 3rd ed. London: Alexander Moring, De La More Press.

——— and J. P. Hardiman. 1900. *Gazetteer of Upper Burma and the Shan States,* Part I, Volume 1. Rangoon: Superintendent of Government Printing and Stationery.

Shanghai Theatrical College. 1986. *Ethnic Costumes and Clothing Decorations from China.* Hong Kong: Hai Feng Publishing Co. and Chengdu: Sichian People's Publishing House.

Shila, Sarapi. 1993. Palong. *TRI Quarterly,* vol. 17, nos. 3–4, pp. 25–39.

Smith, Martin. 1991. *Burma: Insurgency and the Politics of Ethnicity.* London: Zed Books.

Start, Laura. 1917. *Burmese Textiles from the Shan and Kachin Districts.* Halifax: Bankfield Museum.

Stevenson, H. N. C. 1944. *The Hill Peoples of Burma.* London: Longmans, Green.

Suwanbubpa, Aran. 1976. *Hill Tribe Development and Welfare Programmes in Northern Thailand.* Singapore: Regional Institute of Higher Education and Development.

Symes, Michael. 1827. *An Account of an Embassy to the Kingdom of Ava Sent by the Governor-General of India in the Year 1795.* London: Nicol and Wright.

Thomas, David, and Robert K. Headley. 1970. More on Mon-Khmer Subgroupings. *Lingua,* vol. 25, no. 4, pp. 398–418.

Walker, Anthony R., ed. 1992. *The Highland Heritage: Collected Essays on Upland North Thailand.* Singapore: Suvarnabhumi Books.

Woodthorpe, R. G. 1897. Some Accounts of the Shans and Hill Tribes of the states on the Mekong. *Journal of the Royal Anthropological Institute of Great Britain and Ireland,* vol. 26, pp. 13–28.

Yanghwe, Chao Tzang. 1987. *The Shan of Burma: Memories of a Shan Exile.* Singapore: Institute of Southeast Asian Studies.

Yule, Henry. 1858. *A Narrative of the Mission Sent by the Governor-General of India to the Court of Ava in 1855, with Notices of the Country, Government, and People.* London: Smith, Eider & Co.

INDEX

Christianity, 97. *See also* missionaries
clans (clanship), 9, 11, 12, 37–8, 41, 53
clothing. *See* dress
Communist Party of Burma, 19, 75, 76–7. *See also* communists
communists, 4, 13, 76–8. *See also* Communist Party of Burma

D

Danau, 20
Davies, H. R., 49, 55
De'ang, 21, 60–1, 63. *See also* Benglong
Dehong, 19, 21
Denison University, 61
Di-ang, 1, 21. *See also* Pale, Silver Palaung
Diran, Richard, 13–4, 61, 62, 65
Doi Ang Khang, 1, 15, 81, 83
Doi Lae. *See* Loi Lae
dress, 3, 4, 5, 11, 12, 13, 14, 21–2, 31, 36, 45–72, 83–4, 93. *See also* weaving
drug trafficking, 1, 13, 78, 81, 87, 91–2. *See also* heroin trafficking, opium

E

Ethnic Studies Network, 102
Ethnographical Survey of India, 9

F

Fang District, 1, 79, 84, 95
Field Museum, 62
Forestry Department. *See* Royal Forestry Department
Fraser-Lu, Sylvia, 50

G

Ganjanapan, Anan, 100, 102, 106

Golden Palaung, 1, 5, 7, 9, 12, 13, 14, 20, 21, 22, 23, 26, 42, 53, 55, 57, 61, 65, 71, 76. *See also* Shwe, Ta-ang
Göteborg Ethnographical Museum, 47, 62
Green, James Henry, 14, 61

H

Hansen, Henny Harald, 47
Haw, 81
heroin trafficking, 19, 81. *See also* drug trafficking
Hmong, 81
Hsipaw, 9, 20
Htin, 15
Huai Pong, 79, 84, 95, 96
Human Relation Area Files, 12–3

I

India, 9, 17, 19, 31, 39
Indians. *See* India
Irrawaddy River (Ayeyarwady River), 5, 17

J

James Henry Green Collection. *See* Green, James Henry
Japanese, 74
Jingpho (Kachin), 10, 11, 22, 23, 31, 39, 55, 59, 62, 70
Joint United Nations-Thai Programme for Drug Abuse Control in Thailand, 81

K

Kachin people. *See* Jingpho
Kachin State, 1, 19, 20, 22, 23